BASIC TEXTS IN COUNSELLING AND PSYCHOTHERAPY

Series editor: Stephen Frosh

This series introduces readers to the theory and practice of counselling and psychotherapy across a wide range of topic areas. The books appeal to anyone wishing to use counselling and psychotherapeutic skills and are particularly relevant to workers in health, education, social work and related settings. The books are unusual in being rooted in psychodynamic and systemic ideas, yet being written at an accessible, readable and introductory level. Each text offers theoretical background and guidance for practice, with creative use of clinical examples.

Published

Invitation to authors

The Series Editor welcomes proposals for new books within the Basic Texts in Counselling and Psychotherapy series. These should be sent to Stephen Frosh at the School of Psychology, Birkbeck College, Malet Street, London, WC1E 7HX (email s.frosh@bbk.ac.uk)

Basic Texts in Counselling and Psychotherapy
Series Standing Order ISBN 978-0-333-69330-8
(outside North America only)

You can receive future titles in this series as they are published by placing a standing order. Please contact your bookseller or, in the case of difficulty, write to us at the address below with your name and address, the title of the series and the ISBN quoted above.

Customer Services Department, Macmillan Distribution Ltd
Houndmills, Basingstoke, Hampshire RG21 6XS, England

REFLEXIVITY IN THERAPEUTIC PRACTICE

FRAN HEDGES

palgrave
macmillan

First published 2010 by
PALGRAVE MACMILLAN

Palgrave Macmillan in the UK is an imprint of Macmillan Publishers Limited,
registered in England, company number 785998, of Houndmills, Basingstoke,
Hampshire RG21 6XS.

Palgrave Macmillan in the US is a division of St Martin's Press LLC,
175 Fifth Avenue, New York, NY 10010.

Palgrave Macmillan is the global academic imprint of the above companies
and has companies and representatives throughout the world.

Palgrave® and Macmillan® are registered trademarks in the United States,
the United Kingdom, Europe and other countries.

ISBN 978-0-230-55308-8   ISBN 978-1-137-12293-3 (eBook)
DOI 10.1007/978-1-137-12293-3

A catalogue record for this book is available from the British Library.

A catalog record for this book is available from the Library of Congress.

CONTENTS

LIST OF FIGURES

ACKNOWLEDGEMENTS

As I was writing the book I often described it as a hymn of praise, a devotional poem or a love song. As I wrote, I was paying tribute to clients with whom I have been privileged to talk and whose stories had moved me, colleagues and friends to whom I wanted to show gratitude and academics and therapists whose ideas were inspirational.

I would especially like to express appreciation to my supervisor, colleague and friend, Peter Lang, who kept me connected to beautiful ideas. Many of these can be read in these pages.

Thanks to Frances Shaw for the original impetus for the book. Huge thanks for stimulating, irreverent conversations and many laughs through the toughest of times must go to Heleni Andreadi, Karen Barnett, Marybeth Mendenhall, Sanet Marais, Lena Sabass, Dorothea and Martin Miksits, Claire Brockwell, Rebecca Thompson, Lisa Walters and Mark Chidgey.

I would also like to thank Catherine Gray for help with the structure of the book and much, much more, and Stephen Frosh for words of encouragement and further help with structure.

Thanks too to Dr Subrata Banerjea. And a special thank you to Moffie Hamilton.

FOREWORD

This is a very well conceived and beautifully written book. I say "well conceived" because it organizes and integrates so much that is central to systemic therapy and does so around an idea central to the human communication process, "reflexivity."

I want to take a bit of space at the start to address potential readers who are not therapists. I have in mind faculty in Communication, Sociology, Psychology, Management, and other disciplines that include a systemic outlook. I especially commend it to new academics attracted to the social constructionist orientation and who are curious about how it relates to ideas from other perspectives. Perhaps you have picked up this book because of a theoretical interest in communication. Or perhaps you have an interest in the psychology of emotion, language, or embodiment, and see some of these terms in the table of contents. I want to say to you very strongly: read this book! The elegance of its organization and the soundness of its theoretical perspective combine to make it an important contribution to all those of us who count ourselves as part of the "systemic community." In addition, the clarity of writing makes it an excellent "port of entry" for those who are new to this outlook.

In what follows I want to speak briefly about the way this book is organized, for that is one of its great strengths. I call attention to how its sophisticated systemic–pragmatic understanding of communication unifies the work. Second, I will discuss its relevance to three of the most important issues in systemic–pragmatic inquiry, and in the larger social constructionist tradition. Finally, I comment on what I think of as a "double approach" to bringing ideas together in the final two chapters.

Each chapter begins with a theoretical treatment from a pragmatic–systemic point of view, supported by ideas from prominent therapists in this tradition. Specific ideas that are the focus of each chapter are elaborated in an extended case exemplar. As we read the case, we are taken through the process by which Fran Hedges makes choices. She articulates the principles she is using and their intellectual heritage, then transforms them into therapeutic practice. Throughout the book, concepts from the systemic–pragmatic perspective are compared to ideas from other perspectives. This is done in a way that seeks connections whenever possible. That is not to say that the author ignores sharp distinctions when that is necessary. For example, she clearly contrasts her views with Freud's notion of the therapist as a mirror. She makes especially interesting connections between the systemic view and the traditional ideas of "transference," "counter-transference," and "empathy."

I think most readers will be drawn in as I was by the richness of case materials and the experience of joining with a first-rate mind as she works her way through those cases. Fran Hedges draws on her extensive experience in a range of settings as therapist, teacher and supervisor. Often these case reports involve work with her colleague and the reader learns much about how such a professional relationship can enhance reflexive abilities.

I said above that "reflexivity" is central to understanding what is distinctive about communication. This book recognizes that communication is not just another word for interaction. Two computers interact. One sends information to another and the other responds within the parameters of its hardware and software. Living things interact in a more complex way, and all living things interact. They are alive because they are in a relationship of mutual adaptation and accommodation with other living and non-living things. However, human communication is much more than that. John Dewey (1916, 1925) recognized that when children learn to communicate they learn a process that is more than a response to a signal, and more than accommodation and adaptation to their environment. The child learns to "take an interest" (Dewey, 1916) in a special way, a reflexive way. A human child is able to identify itself as an object in space to which others direct their actions. This special ability is shared by few other creatures. A child also learns that her own actions not only affect others, but also affect the way others respond to her. This is the origin of human community. It is a reflexive process and a co-creative process. As a child develops facility with language inside this reflexive process (Meredith Williams, 1999), the child learns to tell "a story" for itself and others about participation in this process, a reflection on the reflexive process. Within this process new ways of thinking, acting, feeling, recalling, and attending are created and re-created.

Once one is committed to this reciprocal, co-construction view of communication, the careful consideration of time becomes intrinsic to the way one works. I have been often struck by the fact that students of communication, therapy, and organizations who know theoretically that time is intrinsic to understanding the social construction process, often fall back upon a time-static description that makes the creation of a useful working hypothesis difficult. I am also taken by the fact that sometimes simply organizing events in time opens new horizons. Many years ago, John Dewey (1925, ch. III) cautioned inquirers of all disciplines about the danger of treating reflection on a process in such a way that the evolving nature of the process is obscured. He reminded his readers that a reflection is itself an occurrence at a particular moment in time. Fran Hedges takes the temporal implication of her pragmatist view of communication seriously. In Chapter 3 she does this in two ways. She shows by means of an extended case example how focusing on the sequential development of communication practices in episodes between a husband and wife provides important understandings. Such understandings are often obscured by time-static reports such as, "She is inattentive," or "He is not protective." The author uses elements of the communication theory "Coordinated Management of Meaning," to show what can be learned from close attention to the sequential co-construction of such ideas about self and other in specific episodes. The reader will also appreciate how the author illustrates the importance of timing (*kairon*) for making therapeutic moves. That is, for deciding what insights to act upon, when, and how. This central understanding of communication runs consistently through the book as the author examines topics such as selfhood, emotion, embodiment, and language.

Earlier, I stressed the value of this book for a wide audience because it addresses three persistent issues in social theory. These issues concern more traditional "stay at home" academics as well as practitioners in the field. By "stay at home" academics, I mean those social scientists in the academy who prefer staying in the office and examining scalar data to getting into connection with the rich and messy details of how people live. The first issue is the problem of connecting micro- and macro-analysis. Vivien Burr (2003) argues that the micro–macro problem is perhaps the most serious one confronting social constructionist work. The second issue is how to reconcile recognition of our own participation in the process of inquiry with a commitment to rigorous standards. This is an old issue originally recognized by Aristotle in his *Nicomachean Ethics*. Said another way, is it the case that the more we understand the influence of what we bring to the situation of inquiry, the weaker our claims must be? The third issue is that of supporting the validity of claims made in qualitative research generally. I will not address "reliability" here because validity is the real goal. The most dedicated quantitative researcher will tell you that there is no reason to care about reliability except to achieve validity. What means do we have that compete with the arsenal of validity tests the positivists have at their disposal?

Let me first address the significance this book has for the micro–macro problem. I am not claiming that Fran Hedges has put this issue to rest, but I do think she has given us some important insight into it, most directly in Chapters 1, 3, 5, and 8. The influence of Cultural Studies, particularly in the American permutation, has had, in my view, a positive as well as negative influence. On the positive side it has encouraged us to recognize that all relationships, families, organizations and individuals live in a larger social system that pre-dates them. There are powerful discourses about race, and gender, as well as about success, responsibility and wealth, that are factors in persons' lives. On the negative side, the Cultural Studies movement has at times encouraged inquirers to treat the rich detail of lived experience as epiphenomenal, that is, as surface manifestations of more important universal forces. This can lead to treating subjects and clients as cultural dopes who do not "really get it." Academics who want to make a difference in the world increasingly self-identify as "public intellectuals," and worse as saviors of "the people" who cut beneath ideology to reveal what is "really" going on. Those of us who disclaim conducting inquiry from a stance of superiority and reject the application of totalizing views to every problem are now often charged with being uncaring and obstructionist. We are supposed to be too stuck in detail to see the "real picture." If you, the potential reader, have a tendency to think that way, read these case analyses!

In Chapter 1, Fran Hedges creates a triad delineating "Grand Narratives," "Big (professional) Stories," and "Personal Stories." She recognizes, as all serious-minded inquirers do, the important role that discourses about selfhood, race, gender and economic factors have in social life. Also recognized as important are Big Stories, including professional stories concerning our position and responsibilities to the client. First, she treats Grand Narrative and Big Stories as *relational* stories, stories about the connection of the therapist (we may include other kinds of professional relationships) to clients. Thus, a Big Story may be about the dominated housewife *and* the liberating therapist, or the over-stressed provider and comforting professional. She shows by means of extended case accounts how reflecting on one's own "Big Story" may be influencing the work, sometimes inhibiting curiosity about the lived experience of the client. This leads her to a set of guides for reflection on the roles therapists' and clients' Big Stories have on the process of therapy. These suggestions are not difficult to extend to other aims of inquiry.

Her second move is to draw upon her knowledge of the philosophy of language. Following Wittgenstein's (1953) later philosophy of meaning, the author avoids treating Grand Narrative and Big Stories as representations of objective reality. She recognizes that grammars of race, gender, ethnicity, and the like are influential as they may become elements of a person's stories about many other things including stories about personal identity, relationship, community and more. She also shows that *if* these words do enter into stories relevant to her work, their function in those stories (their meaning) will not be identical across clients. They will enter into the client's and the clinician's grammars of practice in many different ways. Gender, for example, may be highly relevant to a particular case, but "gender" (as most Cultural Studies advocates would agree) is a social construction. If so, "gender" is a term that points us to a variety of grammars that have "family resemblances," not a universal underlying core. Thus, Fran Hedges recognizes that, as Douglas Adams put it somewhere in his *Hitchhiker's Guide to the Galaxy* series, "Life is complicated and it's not for the timid." Different elements of our learning inform different episodes of practice. Sometimes a couple's problems are related to constructions that are much more local in character and are not best understood as only manifestations of larger discursive formations. Indeed, if we cannot understand the local use of words like "identity," "race," "support" and the like, then we cannot explain how Big Stories are reconstituted in lived experience.

I want to turn to the second issue I identified in social constructionist work. That is, how can we reconcile rigor with acknowledgment of our own participation in the process? During the "Great Paradigm Debate" that occupied social researchers in the academy in the 1970s, it became acceptable, even fashionable, to say that one is not an objectivist. However, that has often been more of a mantra than a family of new methods. Fran Hedges' book is squarely in the tradition of philosophical Pragmatism, which seeks a third position, "Beyond Objectivity and Relativism" (Bernstein, 1985). Fran argues against the old Freudian goal of totally removing the prejudgments and experience of the clinician from the process of therapy. But need this lead us into relativism and finally solipsism? Many academics and some clinicians fear that engaging in reflexive examination of one's own participation raises that specter. What her case examples offer us is not only a more ethically responsible way of working, but a way that provides a greater richness of learning. Thus, recognition of how the inquirer/therapist is connected to others becomes a *positive resource, not a limitation.*

In Chapter 6, which focuses on embodied responsiveness, she describes how her initial response to a client's husband could be described as "bewitchment" by a common cultural story. The husband's imposing physical presence and the couple's initial description of their lives together seemed to fit commonplace stories about inattentive men who withdraw into their own work. Her bodily responses both to the husband's presence and style, and to the wife's weeping, first evoked personal and professional experiences that limited her perspective. They called forth sympathy for the wife and therapeutic efforts to find ways for the couple to re-create their relationship through the husband's greater involvement. The responses to her questions at first seemed to confirm the good fit between this case and the socially/culturally common stories. However, little change was observed. Concerned about possible bewitchment by her prejudices, the author focused on a particular feature of one of the husband's utterances. He used the phrase "I'm a pain" to describe how he felt in certain episodes with his wife. Describing the experience, he showed how he hurt. This evoked a different and vivid bodily response from Fran. The husband's response did not fit the "Big Story." Fran's new questions invited information from him that completely changed her understanding and way of working. Her work in this case enriches our understanding of variety of ways that persons who love each other may protect their relationship. Fran provides the reader with additional insights into *how* we join with others. Thus, the reader is not left with this unpleasant question: "Yes, as inquirers we are full, embodied participants inside the process of inquiry, so – now what do we do?" At the end of each chapter she provides practical guidance to help in this process.

How does this book relate to the issue of generality of case work? Those of us who do case study research are frequently confronted with this charge: If you do not believe that there is a hidden truth revealed by case work, than what kind of contribution to knowledge can case work make since the next case will not be but another reflection of the truth found in the first? Much ink has been spilled over this matter. What Fran Hedges shows is how generalizations about methodology can be claimed *if* the inquirer (therapist, consultant, or others) writes case study reports that: (1) state the principles guiding the work; (2) locate those principles in their philosophical and theoretical orientations; (3) show the relationship of those principles to ideas in other professional discourses; (4) describe how principles are translated into the details of practice; and (5) assess how practices informed the progress of the work. Fran Hedges does all five of these things in each chapter. For example, when she discusses selfhood and identity the reader is given a sound overview of the social constructionist perspective on self and identity, citing the most important contributors. Comparisons and contrasts are made to other perspectives. Then, through detailed accounts of a case, we are shown how the ideas are transformed into specific questions relevant to the information about the particular case. We learn how choices were made in the course of therapy and how these choices were theoretically informed. We are shown how the ideas in action influenced the course of therapy. Now, what could be a stronger "validity" test of an idea "operationalized" than that of real-world observable outcomes? There is a strong family resemblance between this and "predictive validity," the strongest kind of validity, according to the positivist tradition. Notice that these "validity tests" are conducted over and over in the course of case work as ideas about the case evolve.

The last two chapters offer overviews and further development from two different vantage points. In Chapter 7, the vantage point is from new cases, ideas, and suggestions that further develop what has been introduced in other chapters. The reader will be interested in how Fran Hedges develops the connections between the long-standing "problem of translation" in social theory, and a therapist's need to make connections with clients whose experience (cultural, social, or personal) are very different from his or her own. Another theme developed in Chapter 7 will, I think, become of increasing importance to therapists and to the research community in general. That is, how to take seriously "pain" and physical–neurological changes that result from illness or injury. I say this will be a growing concern as increasing numbers of veterans returning from the wars in the Middle East attempt to reconnect with their families and return to work and school.

Chapter 8 returns to many of the book's earlier themes but develops them in a different context, that of the supervisory relationship. Here, too, we are given theoretical background with extended case applications. There are important discussions of how Grand Narratives of class and cultural difference can enter into the social construction of a supervisory relationship. The earlier treatment of the social construction of self is developed further from the viewpoint of the supervisor–supervisee relationship. We are shown how the author uses reflexive ideas to work with trainees' sometimes problematic stories. Many of us have encountered the student who resists learning an important technique by saying, "That is not me. Doing that is not who I really am." Here a student's Big Story is about a "core 'authentic' self," inviting a sympathetic understanding of what cannot be changed. The reader will be very interested in how the author deals with such situations.

In Chapter 8, Fran Hedges also gives a very interesting account of those situations in which there appears to emerge an "isomorphism" between the supervisor–clinician relationship, and the clinician–client relationship. Working from Fruggeri's insight that there can be no real isomorphism, Hedges brings to bear the insights of a reflective position. She examines the institutional, professional, and personal stories that may account for such an observation – in other words she examines with her trainee the social construction of parallel processes – then works on a more productive reframing of the relationships by examining in rich detail the unique participation of all three parties.

Obviously, I very much appreciate this book. You, the reader, must have expected that from the start. But this sensitive, detailed, and well crafted book really does deserve the attention of all those interested in the principles and practices of therapeutic case work.

References

Bernstein, R. (1985) *Beyond Objectivity and Relativism* (Philadelphia: University of Pennsylvania Press).

Burr, V. (2003) *Social Construction*, 2nd edition (London: Routledge).

Dewey, J. (1916/1966) *Democracy and Education* (New York: Macmillan).

Dewey, J. (1925) *Experience and Nature* (Chicago: Open Court Publishing).

Williams, M. (1999) *Wittgenstein: Mind and Meaning* (London: Routledge).

Wittgenstein, L. (1953) *Philosophical Investigations*, trans. G. E. M. Anscombe (New York: Macmillan).

VERNON CRONEN
Massachusetts
August 2009

INTRODUCTION

Doing therapy is an ethically responsible activity and the relationships we form with people who come to us for help can have powerful and far-reaching effects. As we strive to make these conversations useful for people, 'mistakes, humour, and misunderstandings' abound (John Burnham 2005: p. 16). Reflexivity offers both a stance and a range of skills to help us to explore the complexity of what is happening in these conversations so that they can become truly therapeutic.

Throughout my varied career working with homeless people, with people in a psychiatric hospital setting, in the probation service and doing therapy in a higher education context I have been fascinated by the different ways that practitioners talk about their clients. And I have noticed that different practitioners' clients had very different outcomes. It was as if they were drawing from different client groups, despite random referral processes. Some saw their clients several times a week over a long period; some did mainly brief therapy; some made frequent referrals to psychiatrists, whilst some did not; some had many clients with 'attachment' issues, others had clients with difficulties in their families. What could be happening?

I was amused by an idea put forward by one therapist who said that some mysterious force was at work whereby clients were 'attracted' to the kind of therapist they 'needed', and vice versa: 'you get the clients you need', he said. There are, I believe, more mundane communication processes at work which reflexive practices can help us understand. We can identify what makes some conversations useful for clients and some less than useful. In my own practice, for example, I have noticed that when I try to 'understand' too quickly, then the client and I become disconnected.

Doing therapy is a morally responsible activity that involves co-creating meanings with people many of whom are vulnerable. These conversations can be life-changing.

James Griffith and Melissa Elliott Griffith (James Griffith, Melissa Elliott Griffith and Lois Slovik 1990) describe their work with Janet and Dawn, two women who presented separately to a hospital out-patient clinic with ongoing, severe headaches. The outcome of treatment for both women was very different and hospital staff described the two patients as having different personalities: one was seen as 'compliant', the other as 'difficult'. But, Griffith and Elliott Griffith say, the differences between them were actually minimal: it was the way that they worked with each woman that co-created these differences. With Janet, the least liked and least 'successful' patient, 'we studied the headaches, the patient, the family and its interactions. . . . Metaphorically we were hunters stalking a fox.' With Dawn, 'we slowly constructed together a language about the problem that was meaningful to all participants in the problem – myself, Dawn, her mother and husband and sisters, our reflecting team, and the unit nursing staff . . . we came to know the identity of Dawn and her family . . . we were more like the Little Prince with his fox, learning together the rites of taming' (pp. 25–6).

Reflexivity: definition and scope

The *Oxford English Dictionary*'s (1989) definition of 'reflexive' is 'capable of turning or bending back . . . directed back upon the mind itself' (p. 476). The 'self', as George Herbert Mead (1934) says, 'is socially constructed in our everyday social encounters with others and is reflexively involved in its experiences' (p. xxi).

'Reflexivity is an important concept with a wide currency in contemporary thought,' Celia Hunt and Fiona Sampson (2006) say in their excellent book about the self and reflexivity in writing (p. 3). In social science research it is seen as the ideal stance: researchers are urged to reflect on how they construct meanings (David Nightingale and John Cromby 1999, p. 228); anthropologists are expected to reflect on the way they influence their research subjects and vice versa, no longer assuming that they can be neutral observers (Charlotte Aull Davies 1999). Reflexivity helps teachers to re-examine their own frames of reference and helps learners to unlearn their previous assumptions (Donna Qualley 1997).

Reflexivity in therapeutic practice involves complex reciprocal processes: each of us has a range of presuppositions that inform what we notice and don't notice about a client. Reflexivity helps us reflect on what we could be communicating through our emotional responses and language (including bodily languages: clothes, gestures, tone of voice, images, rituals and physical space and so on), what this could be inviting and what we could be co-creating in the process. We become curious (Gianfranco

Cecchin 1987) about what kinds of conversations we are inviting our clients into and what kinds of communication patterns we are co-creating.

Reflexivity is a stance that we take towards the patterns we are co-creating when we communicate as well as being a set of practical skills and abilities that we can use. Reflexivity involves 'reflection-in-action' and 'reflection-on-action' (Donald Schon 1987). In therapy the first, being reflexive during the therapeutic conversation, is challenging for those who work alone, especially beginning therapists. The second involves reflecting afterwards on the patterns we have co-created in the conversation and how our style, language and emotions have affected the client. This helps us prepare for future therapeutic conversations.

Therapists who are fortunate enough to work with a colleague or a team have more opportunity to develop a reflexive stance. A colleague can help us reflect on our biases and interactive patterns and whether we have ignored an important aspect of the client's identity, such as their gender or culture, the areas or topics we are not exploring, whether our presuppositions are useful, if they are making no impact or if they have become a tyranny.

Video-taping or audio-taping therapy conversations can also help us identify helpful and less helpful patterns and we can reflect on the effect of our fleeting, micro-level communications on the client. Therapists can use the tapes in creative ways, viewing them with the client and asking them for feedback on the process. Writing a transcript also helps us develop reflexive practices: we can reflect on the conversation as we write it and again when we discuss it with a supervisor. Talking with colleagues and our supervisor can also expand our own range of stories. As Gianfranco Cecchin et al. (1992) say, we maintain curiosity towards our prejudices 'by maintaining a continuous conversation with colleagues, people outside the mental health field, students, and patients alike' (p. 9). Anything that widens our worldview, such as having conversations with people who come from a different class, culture, area, or country, can help us extend our perspectives and develop multiple positions.

It is often easier to notice the way another therapist is influencing the conversation in a helpful or an unhelpful way.

I recall doing supervision in a small group. A woman therapist called Julie asked for help following a tricky conversation with Sherri, a woman who was bringing up six children single-handedly. I became puzzled about the 'over-helpful' style and jaunty tone of voice I heard Julie using on the audio tape, which was different from her usual style and seemed to belie the seriousness of what Sherri was saying about her life.

After some discussion another therapist in the group observed that Julie's strong identity as a 'good mother' to her only child could be influencing her in some way. Julie made a connection with one of her family stories: her parents had had eight children and, being the eldest, Julie helped her mother care for the younger children; she had resented this position and wanted her own daughter to have a different experience. She realised that she was identifying with Sherri's eldest daughter, rather than being curious about Sherri's position. She made the connection that her 'helpful' style reflected her wish to advise Sherri as she, in hindsight, wished she could have advised her own mother. This brief conversation helped her to notice the differences between her own position and Sherri's daughter's and to hear Sherri's unique stories.

Self-reference and resonance

Our own stories inevitably orient us to notice some things in our therapeutic conversations and ignore, or miss, other things. The two interrelated concepts of 'resonance' and 'self-reference', developed by Mony Elkaim (1990), show this process in action and are immensely useful for reflexive therapists. Elkaim draws on 'constructivist' debates about the subjective nature of the co-construction of 'reality' (Heinz von Foerster 1984; Humberto Maturana and Francisco Varela 1987).

> Whilst we act as if there were a world outside of ourselves – Whose outlines we can quietly describe . . . a territory that we can calmly map . . . this objectivist position is untenable when it comes to psychotherapy. . . . The distinctions that we make are always self-referential, that is each of us constructs our own personal version of reality. (p. xix)

> All the descriptions we make, the aspects we notice about a client's story all relate to what we already know; we inevitably make connections with our own experiences, descriptions and explanations when we meet another person and hear their stories. This means that what we say about a client says as much about ourselves as about them. (p. 74)

A client's story can resonate with one of our own in the way that a 'string' vibrates and reverberates to a similar sound; this can be a powerful experience involving bodily responses, thoughts, feelings and emotions. Resonance can be an invaluable tool if used appropriately and sensitively and can help us create a unique bridge between ourselves and the client.

Co-creating meanings

All stories that people tell are *made* in conversations with others; 'reality' is not simply 'given' to us, it is continuously and reflexively co-constructed (Barnett Pearce 1994). When people meet they influence each other in subtle and profound ways, co-creating unique patterns of communications in what John Shotter (2004) calls 'relationally-responsive' processes. Much that goes on in these communications with others goes unnoticed because we take so much for granted. Austrian philosopher Ludwig Wittgenstein's (1953) revolutionary and practical approach explores the role of language in creating 'reality' and ways that we are 'bewitched' by language when we communicate, and is an inspiration for reflexive therapists. He asks us to pay attention to the unnoticed, fleeting and taken-for-granted aspects of human interaction that go on in the background all the time. As Norwegian therapist Tom Andersen (1996) says, 'The life we as therapists are . . . interested in comprises meanings and feelings which shift all the time . . . they are there for a second and have passed by the next second' (p. 119). Sociologist Harold Garfinkle (1967) refers to 'seen but unnoticed' novel and unrepeatable events (p. 7), and the Russian philosopher Mikhail Bakhtin (1993) talks about events that are occurring for yet 'another first time' (p. 1, in John Shotter 2005: p. 182). Rom Harré (2006) observes that many of Wittgenstein's ideas were anticipated by developmental psychologist Lev Vygotsky (p. 246). Vygotsky's (1962; 1978) observational experiments show how children develop through interaction with adults; children, he says, 'practice . . . the same forms of behaviour that others formerly practiced with respect to him . . . *we become ourselves through others*' (1966: pp. 43–4).

Reflexivity encourages therapists to be endlessly fascinated by the process of co-creating meanings and the complex ways in which each person comes to describe 'reality'. For therapists, reflexive practices enable us to take a position of doubt towards our own biases, making us uncertain about our own certainties and irreverent towards what we may view as unassailable beliefs and prejudices (Cecchin et al. 1992; 1994). We thus develop 'irony towards the discourse' (Roz Leppington 1991). These approaches can help therapists choose the descriptions that are most useful and best 'fit' the particular person at that particular time in that particular context. As we notice the client's responses and check whether they do or do not fit, this helps us question our own dearly-held ideas.

Therapists' internal discourses

Mikhail Bakhtin (1981) refers to the way that healthy development involves a struggle with 'authoritative discourses', which people transform as they 're-write' and 're-tell' them. When a person hears something new, he says, an intense interaction and a struggle with other internally persuasive discourses begins (p. 346). As well as finding ways to help clients transform hurtful authoritative discourses into hopeful ones, therapists are constantly challenging our own internally persuasive discourses, as we talk with clients.

Reflexive positioning, Fathali Moghaddam (1999) says, is the way that we tell ourselves stories in internal conversations, to 'explain' our actions and prepare to tell our story to someone else.

Both concepts show that we are constantly exploring different ways of describing what we are doing, struggling with authoritative discourses and reflexively positioning ourselves in our internal conversations as we reflect on our interactions with other people. We can use these ideas with clients to help them challenge less affirmative descriptions and we can use them to develop stories about our own abilities and professional identity.

'Common sense', presuppositions, 'grand narratives' 'Big Stories' and other prejudices

We are all steeped in our own views of the world and, as influential ecologist and anthropologist Gregory Bateson (1979) notes, all experience is subjective; 'objectivity is impossible'. Indeed, the most unnoticed aspect of our social lives is what he calls presuppositions; we depend on presuppositions to make sense of the world and 'our brains make images that we think we "perceive"' (p. 38). Presuppositions are the 'taken for granted' of our worlds; they are what we consider 'normal' and are often described as 'common sense'. 'Science, like art, religion, commerce, warfare, and even sleep, is based on *presuppositions*' (p. 32).

Many people think that common sense is not cultural at all, says anthropologist Clifford Geertz (1983), but 'contrary to this (commonsensical) idea . . . common sense . . . [is] a cultural system, a loosely connected body of belief and judgement . . . ' (p. 10).

To us, science, art, ideology, law, religion, technology, mathematics, even . . . ethics and epistemology, seem genuine enough genres of cultural expression to lead us not to ask (and ask, and ask) to what degree other peoples possess them . . . what form do they take, and . . . what light has that to shed on our own versions of them. (p. 92)

For example, Americans approach intersexual, or hermaphrodite people with horror; 'common sense is at the end of its tether'. The Navaho tribe, however, view them as divinely blessed, bringing good luck and riches, whilst the East African tribe of Pokot regard them as simple errors, 'like a botched pot', saying that 'God made a mistake' (pp. 82–3). Such presuppositions are simply cultural and historically-specific prejudices. And as Cecchin et al. (1994) say, just as one cannot not communicate, one cannot not have prejudices (p. 29). Indeed, 'therapy takes place in the interplay of the prejudices of therapist and client' (p. 8).

Stories of common sense have 'An air of "of-courseness," a sense of "it figures" ', according to Clifford Geertz, and are seen as 'inherent in the situation', having 'intrinsic aspects of reality'. But as 'a frame of thought common sense is as totalizing as any other' (1983: pp. 84–5). When we maintain that certain descriptions are 'common sense' or 'natural', they are 'thin' descriptions. By 'thin' he means 'simple' or 'literal' (p. 90). We can expand 'thin' stories by exploring more and more details of a client's story, thus making them 'thicker', narrative therapist Michael White (1997) says.

Sooner or later 'our prejudices reveal themselves, whether we want them to or not. They seep through our pretences, coming out in our relationships with others – revealed more by what we do than what we say' (Cecchin et al. 1994: p. 29). These micro-communications are ways that we can 'leak' information through minute facial expressions about how we feel (Paul Ekman and Wallace Friesen 1975), and clients can pick up these minute bodily gestures.

A story is told about a female therapist who wondered why her male client seemed so restrained. Eventually when she asked him how he was experiencing the therapy, particularly her, he said that he sometimes felt uncomfortable. Exploring this further she heard that he found it disconcerting when she made a particular expression with her mouth. When she asked family members they confirmed that sometimes her mouth turned down; so she observed herself in the mirror and noticed when she made this expression so she could change it.

In the 'helping' professions, presuppositions are what Cecchin et al. (1994) call 'Big Stories', which can become 'self-perpetuating, symmetrical escalations' in client–therapist patterns of interaction. Some, like the 'Wounded Therapist', and the 'Missionary Therapist', are, they say, 'powerful and common' prejudices that can have un-therapeutic effects on clients (pp. 9–10). 'If therapists can view their models, hypotheses, and techniques as prejudices rather than unquestionable facts, they are less likely simply to attempt to force these biases on to others.' Even 'strongly held beliefs – such as that loving children is better than ignoring them, or that co-operation is better than fighting . . . can be put on the table for examination, if not with the client at least with one's colleagues . . . ' (p. 15).

We cannot avoid presuppositions and prejudice and indeed they can be useful, claims philosopher Hans Georg Gadamer (1987). Since all understanding is interpretive and involves an exchange between the familiar and the alien, prejudices, 'pre-judgements' or 'fore-structures' can help us make a connection with another person; they are a way of opening us up to be understood. But when we do therapy it is important to be willing to jettison them if and when they don't 'fit' for the client. One important way of practising reflexivity is to invite clients to help us question our presuppositions, 'Big Stories' and prejudices so we can connect to their unique meanings.

Self-fulfilling prophecy and labelling theory

Sociologist Robert K. Merton (1948) coined the phrase 'self-fulfilling prophecy', based on the 'Thomas theorem': 'If men [sic] define situations as real, they are real in their consequences' (William Thomas and Dorothy Swaine Thomas 1928: p. 572). A self-fulfilling prophecy is initially a *false* definition of a situation, which creates a new behaviour, making the original false conception come 'true'. For instance, a deviant label given to a young person early in life can create a complex set of thoughts, feelings and behaviours that can actually lead to the co-construction of a criminal 'career' (Howard Becker 1973). Afterwards people may say that they 'knew' all along that the young person was a 'wrong un'. As Merton (1948) says, 'the prophet will cite the actual course of events as proof that he [sic] was right from in the beginning' (p. 477).

Similar processes take place in the co-construction of a label in mental illness (Thomas Scheff 1966). Although these processes are highly complex and some of these ideas have been critiqued, recent studies in 'modified labelling theory' appear to bear them out. Bruce Link et al. (1989) describe the way that someone with a mental health diagnosis can develop negative self-perceptions which make them withdraw from society; people who have experienced a mental health episode both anticipate negative reactions and notice people's negative reactions to them. In a prospective two-year study of patients discharged from a mental hospital, Eric Wright et al. (2000) found that stigma was a powerful and persistent force in their lives; social rejection was a constant source of distress, which increased feelings of self-deprecation that, in turn, weakened their 'sense of mastery' (p. 68).

There is an enormous body of evidence that backs up the idea that the expectations of professional helpers can be self-fulfilling prophecies (Gerald G. Smale 1977: p. 86). Because of therapists' power to influence clients' self-descriptions it is important that we pay attention to the kinds of stories we 'notice', 'believe' and perpetuate about our clients and the people in their life. However, we can use these ideas to co-create more helpful stories; if we notice and value a person's competencies we begin a process that leads to them behaving in ways that confirm these descriptions (Mark Hubble et al. 1999).

Ideas from 'appreciative inquiry' (David Cooperrider 1990; Srivastva and Cooperrider 1999), an approach that originally worked with organisations to build on people's capabilities and positive visions, can help therapists identify clients' previously unnoticed abilities and co-create more affirmative self-descriptions and ways of living (Elsbeth McAdam and Peter Lang 2009).

I was pleased when, after three years of therapeutic work, twenty-five-year-old Annie told me a fascinating story. We'd had numerous spirited conversations when I tried to counter the self-critical stories she'd developed during a childhood and adolescence of sexual and emotional abuse. When she told me she was 'bad' and 'a waste of space' I would help her notice her many abilities such as her determination to make a better life for herself and her generosity towards friends. She showed an interest in the theories and concepts I was using, which I would explain.

After she had started to work in a youth project she told me an exciting story: she'd been warned to stay away from an 'unpredictable, aggressive' teenage boy; instead she deliberately introduced herself to him, saying that she'd heard how helpful he was. From that day he was keen to show his helpfulness. She used every opportunity to comment on his abilities and soon other members of staff noticed improvements in his behaviour and attitude. I was thrilled when Annie told me that my persistence in noticing her abilities and the way I explained the theory helped her understand these ideas so she could put them into practice with that 'aggressive' boy.

Therapists' intentions

Because people tend to come to see a therapist when things are not going well, some therapists believe that it is respectful to focus on their difficulties, and this prejudice can influence our therapeutic conversations in subtle and pervasive ways. Kenneth Gergen (1991) refers to this as a 'deficit model' where 'problem-saturated' stories come to obscure other more hopeful ones.

However, research shows that an effective outcome in therapy involves amongst other things a hopeful therapist (Rick Snyder, Scott Michael and Jennifer Cheavens 1999), a focus on the client's personal and external resources and the ways in which they are already changing (Karen Tallman and Arthur Bohart 1999, in Hubble et al. 1999).

As we have seen, we all have presuppositions and prejudices and rather than trying to get rid of them, which is impossible, it is more useful to become interested in our expectations, our intentions and the consequences of the therapeutic choices we make. They can subtly but powerfully shape therapeutic conversations.

We can do this in small ways. For example, I saw Ben, a nine-year-old boy, with his mother and twin sister. Teachers at Ben's school were concerned about his 'disruptive' behaviour in class; they considered a possible ADHD (attention deficit hyperactive disorder) diagnosis and suggested that he be referred to a psychologist. His parents were upset and a mutual friend suggested that they come to see me privately. As I had little knowledge of ADHD I wasn't sure how I could help.

When we met I noticed that while his sister sat calmly Ben constantly moved around, looking everywhere; he seemed like a curious child. He confirmed that he liked being active and playing football rather than sitting in the class-room, although he was bright and was doing well at school. It was the beginning of the conversation and I was checking out how long they expected to be there. When I said it could be an hour or so, Ben's mother immediately replied, 'He won't be able to sit still for that long.' Without thinking, I said, with a grin, 'I think he can.' Amazingly, from that moment Ben stopped wriggling about and became engaged in the conversation. He showed an impressive understanding of how his attempts to be 'helpful' to the teacher were misconstrued as being 'interfering', and he and his sister enjoyed thinking of ways that he could train the teachers to pay less atten-tion to him. The time seemed to fly by and after we had been talking for over an hour I noticed that no-one, including Ben, seemed keen to leave.

From self-awareness to self–other-reflexivity

Reflexivity includes an ability to be 'self-aware' but there is so much more: we are aware of ourselves and how we affect others in an ongoing 'self-reflexive' process. This also involves an appreciation of the rights and responsibilities within the context.

In the previous vignette I had the right to ask questions and explore issues in Ben's life and I had responsibility for conducting an ethical conversation that would help Ben and his family.

Peter Lang's (2003) 'self–other-reflexivity' describes the to-and-fro, back-and-forth process of response–invitation–response involved in the reflexive process. Each person's response is simultaneously an invitation to the other person; a response can validate or refute the other person's presuppositions and prejudices. Since we can never anticipate how the client will interpret a word, phrase, comment or question, a bodily gesture such as a nod, smile, frown or any other communication, it is important for us to be continuously self–other-reflexive by checking out with them how the conversation is affecting them, as we have seen in the example of the client who had difficulty with his therapist's micro-communications. John Burnham's (2005) 'relational reflexivity' is an invaluable tool, particularly for those who work alone, that enables us to check out how the client is experiencing the conversation. By asking for feedback during the conversation we can invite the client into self–other-reflexive conversations and this can help us reflect on how the client is affected by us, so that we can reflect on how our prejudices, language and actions are inadvertently affecting them.

We cannot stand aside from this ongoing process; even saying nothing is a response, and silence can be a powerful communication (Paul Watzlawick 1984).

Peter Lang (2008) talks about therapists developing a 'third eye' to help us shift between the client's position and our own. A 'third eye' perspective gives us a questioning stance towards our presuppositions, biases, emotions and verbal and bodily languages and helps us develop self–other-sensitivities about the effect of the subtlest of our interactions on our clients.

Patterns

Reflexive therapists also pay attention to the *patterns* of interaction we are involved in co-creating, whether they are inspirational, make no difference or are hurtful. Pattern relates to connectedness and is ubiquitous in the natural and the social world, according to Gregory Bateson (1979); being 'responsive to *the pattern which connects*' is an aesthetic appreciation of life (p. 17). Railing against the Cartesian and Newtonian dualism prevalent in Western thought, he says that: 'The damage is the taking apart. The sacredness is the coming together. The sacred is the hook up, the total hook up and not the product of the split' (1991: p. 302).

Bateson's ideas influenced family systems theory, particularly the Milan systemic team, who based their sophisticated model of family therapy on the idea of pattern, relationship and connectedness (Rudi Dallos and Roz Draper 2000; Lynn Hoffman 1981). Every part of a 'system' influences every other part: each person in a family, team, organisation or community affects everyone else in some way.

When a therapist meets a client or family we will inevitably 'join' and influence that 'system'. Working with this idea is known as taking a 'second order' position, a concept drawn from 'cybernetics' and the idea of 'feedback loops'. It was accepted in 'systems theory' and family therapy by the late 1980s. But it has taken time for practice to catch up with theory and many therapists using these approaches still tend to focus on the *clients'* stories and *their* relationships and behaviour: a 'first order' position. If we are serious about developing reflexive practices we will notice the patterns that we are co-constructing with our client; we will take both a 'first order' position to explore clients' stories and patterns in their life as well as a 'second order' position to reflect on what we are co-creating with them.

Therapists can affect many people's lives. We have more influence on the client's worldview than the other way around because of the power of therapists in our culture, so what we say in these conversations involves ethical and moral considerations. We can also influence a client's wider networks of relationships such as members of their family, friends, work colleagues and people in their religious or political community and so on.

Reflexive therapists are also interested in the patterns we are co-creating in our own personal and professional relationships because all these can have a powerful impact on our clients.

Curiosity and irreverence

Reflexivity is closely linked to a posture of 'curiosity' (Cecchin 1987), a revision of the Milan team's concept of 'neutrality' (Maria Selvini Palazzoli et al. 1980). A stance of curiosity helps us to continue to look for different descriptions even when this seems impossible (p. 411). There are always multiple versions of the world (Gregory Bateson 1972: p. 77) and curiosity invites us to consider other versions when one doesn't 'fit' or is not useful. We show that we are losing curiosity and have stopped listening to our client when we become bored and believe we know what is happening, Cecchin (1987) says, or we experience psychosomatic symptoms such as headaches, back ache or perspiration or, for example, fantasise about becoming a plumber, or a waitress (p. 410).

We enhance our curiosity and develop self-reflexivity by becoming 'irreverent' towards dogma, our own sacred cows and accepted 'truths'. Irreverence helps us to become uncertain of certainties and celebrate self-doubt (Cecchin et al. 1992). Doubt, a luxury for people living in some cultural and political contexts, is crucial for reflexive therapists. It 'is useful for therapists always to have a little doubt about what they are believing, what they are seeing, in order to prevent themselves from becoming fanatical and therefore dangerous to their clients' (Cecchin et al. 1994: p. 19). 'In order to be able to attain this ability for self-reflexivity, we believe that it is necessary to have a certain level of irreverence and a sense of humour' (Cecchin et al. 1992: p. 9).

The irreverent therapist 'constantly undermines the patterns and stories constraining the . . . [client], promoting uncertainty . . . '. Doing this enables the client's 'system' to 'evolve new beliefs and meanings and less restrictive patterns'. Therapists must also be willing not to become a true believer in what we are asked to do by the state, or the institution, or even the clinic in which we work (p. 9). Quite a challenge.

For those who long for certainty and theories in which to believe, particularly beginning therapists, these ideas can feel dizzyingly relativistic, as if there is no solid ground. But curiosity and irreverence can mean *consciously* using a prejudice or passionately taking a stand about something, for the time being, as long as we notice the effects of this on the client and others in their life, and, more importantly, if we are willing to alter our position if this does not fit the client or does not create more hopeful stories.

If we acknowledge that there are countless ways of describing 'reality', we can explore other descriptions and explore the unsaid, untold and unnoticed aspects of clients' stories. We cannot 'understand' another person 'fully' or 'know' what life is like from their position, but we can work creatively with clients to develop more life-affirming identities, relationships and ways of living.

Karen Partridge (2007) draws a diamond-shaped diagram with clients and supervisees to bring forth unnoticed 'shy' stories, specifically an opposite idea. For example, if a client talks about feeling *out of control* she will explore times when the client feels *in control*, drawing both positions on opposite sides of the 'diamond'. This helps client, therapist and supervisor to become 'reflexively repositioned'. She describes this as 'third order positioning'.

All these ideas involve extending our repertoires of practices. Experimentation and improvisation helps us develop new abilities which moves us into 'a place where novelty and uncertainty hold hands. . . . It is the moment for the sharp intake of breath before the dive . . . ' (Jim Wilson 2007: p. 52).

1

How our Stories Influence Therapeutic Conversations

In this chapter I explore concepts that are called 'common sense'. These presuppositions, professional narratives and personal stories profoundly affect our therapeutic conversations.

Each person is immersed in cultural norms and values which are formed within their specific family, community, historical time and political era. Reflexive therapists value the unique position that each person occupies in the world: physical and bodily differences and what we call the GRRAAC-CCES': gender, race, religion, age, (differing) abilities, culture, colour, class, ethnicity, sexual orientation (John Burnham and Queenie Harris 2002), and so on, which permit or exclude people from certain contexts and encourage the development of specific narratives.

When we meet a client we enter and join their culture; our identities inter-mingle. We develop our 'narrative identity' from the stories others tell about us; we are 'literally entangled in stories at the interpersonal level', French philosopher Paul Ricoeur (in Richard Kearney 1996) says. 'The story of my life is a segment of the story of your life; the story of my parents, of my friends, of my enemies, and of countless strangers' (pp. 6–7). In these ways we participate in each other's cultures and influence each other's self-descriptions, developing what Peter Lang (2007) calls 'we-dentities'. But, by the very nature of the kinds of conversations we have, therapists are more influential in influencing clients' identities than vice versa.

When Barbara rang the University Counselling Service to make an appointment I already 'knew' a lot about her, based on all the stories I had heard during the previous year. Many people were concerned about her and had urged her to seek 'help' from 'a professional' for her 'problems with alcohol'. The stories described Barbara as an isolated student. She had been drinking alcohol alone and had passed out numerous times during lectures and twice had to be escorted home. Other shortcomings and incompetencies were mentioned. Because many people had told Barbara that she should seek 'help' from 'a professional' for 'her problems' a story was being co-created that described Barbara as having 'problems', for which, it was assumed, she 'needed' help from 'a professional'.

Presuppositions, 'grand narratives' and other prejudices

We draw our assumptions, stories and values from culturally available narratives:

(a) 'presuppositions' and 'grand narratives';
(b) 'Big Stories' and professional narratives about 'best practice';
(c) our own personal stories.

These are, of course, artificial distinctions as with any model or typology. 'Grand narratives' usually go unremarked and unnoticed, yet they have become so assimilated into our view of life that they are accepted as 'common sense' and have profound implications for how people come to describe the world. For example, the taken-for-granted Western idea that the 'self' is individual and separate from other selves arises from a 'grand narrative' from a particular political and cultural world; it is simply a prejudice (Geertz 1983).

Therapists not familiar with critiquing 'grand narratives' such as these may ask: Why should we concern ourselves with 'theory' at this level? Surely this doesn't impinge on our work with clients? Yet these concepts do affect our clients in 'real', practical ways, says Michael White (1997). Drawing on Michel Foucault (1988), he says that when we accept these 'grand narratives', they 'make it virtually impossible for us to notice events that don't fit . . . they narrow options for other ways of thinking and stop clients noticing how they participate in creating their own life'.

Because 'the link between knowledge and power is obscured, this decreases therapists' ability to address ethical considerations'. Therapy can reproduce certain 'truths' about human nature and human development, but 'In practice this restricts us and the persons who consult us to deficit-centred or problem-saturated accounts' (pp. 225–30).

'Big' professional stories, Gianfranco Cecchin et al. (1994) say, are 'extremely powerful and common prejudices'. Many therapists share the prejudice of the 'Wounded Therapist'. On the basis of the 'belief that

people need . . . warmth, understanding, and, at times, even love', a therapist who accepts this prejudice as a truth sees a client as 'someone who has
received faulty nurturing and needs a corrective love experience'. However,
the more 'needy' the client becomes, 'the more loving/nurturing the therapist becomes'; the client becomes addicted to the unconditional love from
this therapist and ends up describing themselves as 'like a child whose
judgment is faulty'. The second posture they describe is that of the
'Missionary Therapist', a person who has come from a 'healthy family'
who believes that they know what 'normal is and how a family or individual *should* behave'. The danger is that the therapist can become 'somewhat
of an aristocrat who . . . knows what is best for everyone'. Clients can
become reliant on this 'psycho-educative', authoritative therapist, who co-
creates the incompetent client (pp. 9–12).

Clients and therapists may have similar or different assumptions about
therapy: a client may have the idea that 'real' therapy involves talking about
their problems and this prejudice may be shared by the therapist. Another
therapist may prefer to explore the client's competencies and abilities; there
are ethical implications regarding which of our own personal and family
stories, cultural presuppositions (Inga-Britt Krause 1998) and 'Big' professional stories we choose, since they can profoundly affect the stories we
notice and co-create with clients.

*Because I worked in the same institution where Barbara was studying, we
were already immersed in relationships that connected us. What others said
or didn't say about me and the service I ran and what they said or didn't
say about Barbara created stories that influenced our relationship: as I
develop stories about Barbara and her identity, she will be developing
stories about me and my identity. Before we met, stories were already being
co-constructed about each other; our identities already becoming entangled.*

*If she has talked in a therapeutic context or has heard about this kind of
'help' this will also influence her. I will be curious about the inner talks
Barbara has with herself about her 'identity', the influential voices from
family and friends that she draws on, the cultural stories in 'the media'.
Similarly I will have developed a range of professional stories from conversations with colleagues and in supervision, through reading therapy texts
and attending workshops and so on.*

*I wondered how I could challenge my least useful presuppositions and 'Big
Stories'. I wanted to be irreverent to the idea that Barbara 'needed' me to
get on with her life, and that I knew what was best for her. It is not that I*

would hold back from offering helpful information, but I would guard against the desire to 'help' Barbara, preferring to explore which model of help fitted best for her. I wanted to listen closely to the unique ways she was responding to life so that our relationship could become therapeutic for her. Also I wanted to question the familiar 'Big' story that Barbara's behaviour meant that she had enduring 'alcohol problems' and that this related to personal shortcomings, rather to be curious about the contexts in which alcohol had become the best response.

Alcohol is seen in our culture as being a normal recreational drug linked to rites of passage, particularly in the student context, and is usually consumed in social groups. However, when young men experiment with alcohol they are described as 'normal', whilst young women often attract criticism.

Barbara arrived on time. I greeted her warmly; one of my prejudices is that being warm and welcoming creates a good context for therapeutic work. When we went into the room she sat down in an upright, rather formal way, her eyes lowered. A slight, neatly-dressed young woman in her mid-twenties, wearing conservative clothes, she looked at me in what appeared to be a timid way. Her black skin was beautiful.

Barbara was not as I had imagined; she challenged all my preconceptions. It was hard to reconcile the trim, softly-spoken person who sat in front of me with the student who had been described as getting drunk and creating so much disruption. Until I met her I didn't realise I'd had such strong prejudices. First I asked her about what hopes she had for the conversation. Speaking quietly she said she wanted to complete her degree. To my question about why she had chosen to come now, she said she was about to go into her third and final year (having had to re-take a year) and wanted to prepare for it.

As Peter Lang (2007) says, 'it is not that we ignore people's difficulties. Rather, we are curious about how the person has *responded to* them'.

I didn't ignore the fact that she might have some struggles and that people were concerned about her (I'd heard that her behaviour had disrupted their classes); but I wanted to be self-reflexive about my presuppositions, the professional 'Big Stories' and my own personal stories that could be organising what I noticed about Barbara.

The danger of focusing on clients' shortcomings cannot be emphasised enough, according to Peter Lang (2007), since what we focus on tends to expand.

It is understandable that other professionals have become concerned about Barbara, but I don't want to focus on these descriptions to the exclusion of others that could fit just as well but be more useful. If I describe her, even to myself, as problematic this will subtly but profoundly affect the direction the conversation takes. But, if I focus on and explore her abilities and capabilities and the small ways that Barbara is making positive changes these descriptions will expand and will influence the stories Barbara comes to tell about herself. I intend to explore Barbara's 'internal' resources, such as her determination to stay on the course, and her 'external' resources, such as any positive family relationships or friendships in her life. Doing this could also help me develop and maintain hopefulness in my work with her.

Clients' strengths, abilities, competencies, resources (personal and in their life) are 'the trump card', 'the winning hand' and *the* most important variables in successful therapy outcome, Hubble et al. (1999) maintain (p. 412).

Unfortunately, most theories of therapy are theories of psychopathology, says Barbara Held (1991). Indeed, 'clients have not been highly regarded in most therapeutic systems'. They are described as 'the maladjusted, disturbed, regressed, neurotic, psychotic, and character-disordered' (in Hubble et al. 1999: p. 409). Unsurprisingly, research shows that therapists rated as less effective by clients showed negative behaviours such as 'belittling and blaming, ignoring and negating, attacking and rejecting' (Ted Asay and Michael Lambert 1999: pp. 34–5). More effective therapists used more positive behaviour, and 'basic capacities of human relating – warmth, affirmation, and a minimum of attack and blame – may be at the center of effective psychotherapeutic intervention' (Najavits and Strupp 1994, in Asay and Lambert 1999: pp. 34–5).

This was the middle of the long summer vacation and it would be about two months before the start of the new academic year. Barbara's tutor has been supporting her; tutors are busy people and do not spend time with every student. Perhaps the tutor saw Barbara as an able student with potential? Instead of only seeing her as a person with problems I have already begun to notice her competencies.

A change focus

When therapists notice that people who come to therapy have already started to make changes this is more likely to lead to a successful outcome (Hubble et al. 1999). They contrast this with the idea of the therapist as 'hero' who sees themselves as the one who will help the client make changes in their life.

If we want to enhance the possibility of a good therapeutic outcome, therapists should adopt 'a change focus' and see change as inevitable, thus casting our clients in the role of *primary* agents of change rather than casting *ourselves* in this position. 'Within the client is a theory of change waiting for discovery . . . ' (p. 431). The distinction is subtle but important: since therapists invest a great deal of time, money and energy developing our abilities and skills, it is understandable that we tend to attribute more importance to what we are doing, rather than what the client is doing.

I had noticed that Barbara was already making positive changes: she had come during the summer vacation and said she wanted to complete her degree. She had made an appointment and had turned up for it, which showed that she had made a decision to do something to make a change in her life. I was developing the idea that she was a highly organised, forward-thinking young woman who was keen to succeed.

The client's view of the relationship

Second to clients' strengths, is the client's view of the therapeutic relationship. 'Therapeutic success depends on enabling and confirming the clients' resources in a partnership informed by the clients' goals and perceptions' (Hubble et al. 1999: p. 418).

There have been some misunderstandings about the therapist–client relationship in systemic therapy but this has always been centre stage for us, says Glenda Fredman (2007). A central concept from Gregory Bateson's (1979) ground-breaking ideas is that when a therapist meets a client their relationship is mutually influential and affects many lives.

These ideas helped me retain awareness of how our conversation could affect not only her but her family, friends, tutors and so on as well as the relationships in my own life.

Suddenly she burst out, 'I've more or less stopped drinking.' I was astounded and nodded and smiled encouragingly.

Barbara rushed on. Last year she'd been drinking 'too much': a bottle of wine every day. What made her choose wine? It was 'easy to buy' she said.

How had drinking helped, I asked. It had helped her 'cope' with 'feeling self-conscious', in lectures, she said. I was puzzled about the meaning of 'feeling self-conscious': in my experience it is the lecturer who is on show. Wanting to lighten the solemn tone of the conversation and put Barbara at ease, I risked a joke about it being a lecturer's job to talk and 'perform' whilst all the student has to do is listen and write notes.

I wondered what she thought about my feeble joke; did it fit with her view of a professional?

'Sometimes you have to speak,' she said. I thanked her and said I remembered now that some lecturers encourage student participation. Had she used other ways to cope, I asked. She said she had been to see a counsellor in an external organisation, but didn't like him and had not gone back. Why was that? I asked. 'Because he just sat there,' she replied. Noticing that Barbara was now responding more easily, I took that to mean that she appreciated my interactive style, even my rather suspect humour.

'Spontaneity, mistakes, humour, and misunderstandings', systemic family therapist John Burnham (2005) says, 'are all part of the uncertain process through which relationships are created' (p. 16). A playful approach to 'serious' issues can enable us to challenge our own ideas and help us create hopeful stories.

Returning to the theme of feeling self-conscious, I began to search for other descriptions: 'un-self-confident', or 'shy'? Barbara shook her head each time and I began to feel rather frustrated and wondered what this could be telling me.

The desire to find a true description of a person is drawn from the Western presupposition that the 'self' is static and it is possible to discover internal aspects of a person's 'real self', which influences the world of psychiatry. For example, psychiatrist Christopher Lane (2007) notes that a wide range of normal reactions, such as shyness, and normal worries, such as fear of eating alone in public and fear of public speaking, were pathologised after being grouped together under the general diagnosis of 'social phobia' in the diagnostic manual, DSM1V, in 1980.

I berated myself for the way I had fallen into these traps and was thankful that she had refused all the descriptions I had been giving. I asked myself why I had not explored her meanings and the contexts in which self-consciousness had come to be co-constructed in Barbara's life. Then I recalled that students who don't talk to other students often have the idea that everyone else is coping easily with academic challenges and that they are the only one who is struggling. Barbara has been described as 'isolated'; did she believe she was the only student to feel self-conscious?

'Speaking in public,' I said, in a casual way, 'is supposed to be the most nerve-wracking thing for most people. Did you know?' Barbara shook her head, looking interested.

'Lots of students say that it's scary speaking in class,' I added. My knowledge of the context and expertise were useful; by 'normalising' her reaction I hoped this would help Barbara realise that she wasn't alone.

I had reflected that my style had become 'too' interactive because her style was so serious and hesitant. As I began to match her style I noticed her becoming more forthcoming.

We are 'polyphonic'

How we speak and what we say is never simply our own; it is always partly someone else's, says Mikhail Bakhtin (1981: p. 345). We are 'polyphonic'; many different voices combine when we talk (1984). Reflexive therapists working alone can bring in the voices of other clients, people from their own life and so on, to expand the voices available in the room.

When I had mentioned other students who had told me how scared they were to speak up in lectures I could see that Barbara enjoyed hearing the new perspectives these voices gave her.

Many voices were influencing me as I talked with Barbara: inspiring clients, therapists, colleagues and trainees, 'theorists' and writers, and drawing on them enabled me to take self-reflexive positions with Barbara.

Now I wanted to hear the influential voices in Barbara's life.

'Who's most proud that you're about to go into your final year?' I asked.

'Mum and dad,' she answered; she told me that her mother was from Barbados and her father was from Jamaica. This gave me an opening to explore other voices in her family.

Her brother and sister had successful jobs, she said; they were 'a close family'. Although she answered willingly she seemed rather bemused by my interest in her family. Everyone was getting on with their lives, she said, they didn't affect her and were of no consequence; they simply lived under the same roof.

I wondered whether Barbara had the idea that it was disloyal to talk about her family, which could 'explain' what she was saying and also her hesitant style. Maybe she thought my questions implied criticism? She described herself as separate from her family. Perhaps she wanted to be 'different' from them whilst at the same time wanting to make them proud of her?

There are strong cultural stories reinforced by 'Big' professional therapy stories that suggest that a young person must 'individuate' from their parents by a certain age. I kept these in mind but wanted to be irreverent to them, preferring to explore the unique way that Barbara's relationships with the important people in her life were influencing her. They could be people from her past, her current life and even those from an imagined future.

I recalled a therapist whose parents came from Jamaica telling me that she felt she had to work much harder than people with white British parents; she'd felt she was always trying to prove herself. This voice was useful.

Barbara told me her parents were 'managers', but she didn't know what they did. She was equally hazy about her brother and sister's profession. I was rather taken aback. Surely, I thought, its 'normal' to have some idea of your parents' occupation? Then I reminded myself that there was no 'normal' way to 'do' family. I didn't want to fall into the trap of being a 'missionary therapist' who 'knows' how people 'should' live, as described by Gianfranco Cecchin et al. (1994). She seemed to be following her family's values of success through hard work: her brother and sister were both successful and high-achieving, as were her parents. I wondered about how drinking fitted with these family values and expectations but for the time being wanted to explore other resources in her life and other voices that could be influencing Barbara's description of herself.

Exploring clients' resources: friendships

The resources that clients have outside therapy are important to a successful outcome in therapy, so strengthening these is crucial (Hubble et al. 1999).

Barbara had made many references to friendship: 'you should make good friends at university', 'friends for life', 'real friends', so now I asked about her friends. Barbara said she was only in touch with one school friend, but she didn't want to be friends with her any longer. I asked why.

'Because she wants to go clubbing' she answered, wrinkling her nose. She'd refused to go with her. I laughed and said I didn't blame her and she shot me a tentative smile.

Recalling the description of her as an isolated student, I wondered whether this was a friendship she could build on and risked putting this idea forward in the form of another joke: 'She's not contagious – just because she enjoys clubbing,' I said.

'I know,' she said, 'but I don't want to go to those places with her.' She gave me a broad grin and visibly relaxed.

I was relieved as I hadn't been sure whether she was finding the style of the conversation useful. Now I began to feel more hopeful. Perhaps my humour was helping us make a good connection?

Barbara said that she wanted friends who were different from her school friends; she wanted to be 'a different kind of person' at university. I became intensely interested.

'What were you like at school?' I asked.

'Flippant, loud and false' she answered.

I was astonished; this challenged my perception of Barbara and it was a description that didn't match the demure person who sat in front of me. How did this new information help make sense of how she was behaving at university?

Psychologist Steve Duck (1983), writing about friendship, describes how people differ enormously in their need for friendship. But, friendships, 'don't just happen . . . they have to be made – made to start, made to work, made to develop, kept in good working order, and preserved from going sour' (p. 9). Geographical closeness *and* the right circumstances combine to help people make friends. This is counter-intuitive to the way we usually think about friendship.

The more fragmented setting of university life with its modular system does not offer the same continuity of relationships as at school. Students who live in halls of residence have more opportunities to socialise and thus make friends, a context that particularly suits those who like going 'clubbing'.

But Barbara lived at home with her family and she didn't want to have the kind of 'flippant' friendships she'd had at school; she was experimenting with a different identity, trying to develop different kinds of friendships. The context in which Barbara was studying was mainly white; the culture of many younger students was a social, drinking one, which didn't suit her. Barbara was black, whilst most students were white; she was slightly older than others, didn't live in halls of residence and didn't enjoy going 'clubbing'. In a context where similarities are valued, Barbara was different from many other students; even a two-year age gap can make a big difference to the way students make friends.

Ethnicity, race, culture and colour are crucial in friendship development: we tend to gravitate towards those who are similar to ourselves. As Steve Duck points out, someone who is having difficulty with making friends is not necessarily personally deficient; they may just be in the wrong place. There are logistical and practical reasons why friendships develop: research has shown that the simple physical location of people's front doors affects friendship patterns: people make friends with neighbours whose front doors face towards each other (Festinger et al. 1950, in Duck 1983: p. 16).

I also wanted to challenge a strong presupposition in our culture that describes a successful person as 'popular' and 'sociable'. People who enjoy their own company are often described as 'loners', 'weird' and even 'unpredictable' and 'dangerous'.

I didn't describe Barbara as personally deficient: for many reasons she simply didn't fit with other students. I explored whether she had any friends at university and she told me about two older students who she didn't see much because they lived a long way from her. Rather than focusing on the idea that Barbara was unsuccessful at making friends, I was developing the idea that she was choosing potential friends from older, possibly more serious, students than her school friends.

'You've made friends here and also you had a lot of friends at school,' I said, 'How would your school friends describe you?'

She said they would describe her as friendly, helpful and loyal. I noticed the way her expression had brightened as we noticed these skills and abilities. 'You've got really good eye-contact,' I said, 'and when you smile your whole face lights up.' She gave me an even more brilliant smile and this made me feel hopeful.

'Repression' in the self-help industry

Then out of the blue she said, 'I've been working on myself.' When I explored this she said she'd been writing a diary, taking herbs, taking more exercise and eating more healthily. All this had helped her not to drink. Again, I was taken aback, in a good way.

Originally Barbara had found a novel way to cope with feeling 'self-conscious' and gain the courage to attend lectures, by drinking wine. When this had ceased to be helpful, she'd tried other ways. I was impressed by her inventiveness and ability to search for solutions.

At the same time I noticed that all the 'self-help' activities she was trying out were solitary. I wondered whether she was being influenced by 'grand narratives' about the 'self' in our culture. The way she talked about 'working on herself' made me wonder whether she had been inspired by the self-help industry.

Self-help literature makes us believe that it is desirable to live a life that is free of repression, and involves 'helping the client become *who they really are*' (White 1997: pp. 221–2). 'Self-help' takes a multiple view of the self, but these voices tend to be seen as 'contaminating . . . the alien voices must be shed to realize a pure, unified self' (Sheila McNamee and Ken Gergen 1999: p. 31).

In honouring the ways that Barbara had been doing this self-work, I was irreverent to the 'grand narrative' that she had a 'true-self' that she was 'liberating' from 'repressive forces' or the familiar idea that a 'successful self' is one that is surrounded by people. She had tried this identity at school and was exploring different ones.

Challenging presuppositions about 'the self'

The Western view of the self is one where 'striving for self-actualization and turning to one's inner self for strength, definition and guidance in dealing with others' is the norm (Geertz 1983).

The idea of a single 'real' or 'true' self, which we are constantly searching for and will someday discover, is part of what has been called the 'grand narrative' of humanism, French philosopher Jean-François Lyotard (2001) says. Such a description is so embedded in our culture, so pervasive and seductive that it is seen as 'truth'. But these are simply assumptions created within a particular culture at a particular historical time (Hunt and Sampson 2006). Fortunately our identity isn't fixed; there are many opportunities to develop our self-descriptions and self-identities through discourses with others (Bakhtin 1981; 1986). Each of us is, in Julia Kristeva's (1984) phrase, a 'subject-in-process'.

Was Barbara turning to her 'inner self' for 'strength, definition and guidance'? I recalled another idea familiar in the West, which is that a successful person resolves things on their own and doesn't 'burden' others with their problems.

If I follow the 'grand narrative' that a successful adult is one who is 'self-sufficient' with a strong 'inner self' or if I describe Barbara, even in my internal conversations, as unsuccessful at making friends, these descriptions will obscure other stories that explore the unique, creative, experimental ways that she is living her life. Instead I described Barbara to myself as a young woman who was in an experimental process of self-development, trying out many different self-identities and ways of living.

The self is co-created in social contexts

'Languages of the self . . . are many,' Jeffrey Stout (1988) maintains, and they are embodied in specific social practices and institutions – religious, political, artistic, scientific, athletic, economic, and so on' (pp. 291–2). For example, the idea that a healthy person should turn to their 'inner self for strength, definition and guidance' is not shared by other cultures. In Western cultures the self is viewed as a

> bounded, unique, more or less integrated motivational and cognitive universe, a dynamic center of awareness, emotion, judgement, and action . . . organized into a distinctive whole and set contrastively both against other such wholes and against a social and natural background. (Clifford Geertz 1975: p. 48, in Pearce 1994: p. 256)

If I am to be useful to Barbara I will question my own cultural presuppositions about what constitutes a successful 'self'. I will be curious about how Barbara's 'self' has been co-created in various social practices and conversations. If I am entranced by, and uncritically accept, the Western taken-for-granted view of the self I might inadvertently reinforce Barbara's belief that she is alone and must 'individuate' from her parents. This could ignore the unique and important voices that have contributed to the co-construction of stories of Barbara's 'self'.

In our conversation Barbara and I are co-constructing our-selves together; I am shifting between different positions, noticing Barbara's stories and also reflecting on my own assumptions and prejudices and how these are affecting my stories and into which kinds of conversations I am inviting her.

REFLEXIVITY IN THERAPEUTIC PRACTICE

Discourses about the self are mired in muddled thinking, claims Rom Harré (1998). The self, 'as the singularity we each feel ourselves to be is not an entity. . . . Rather it is a site . . . a place from which a person perceives the world and a place from which to act. . . . Selves are grammatical fictions, necessary characteristics of person-oriented discourses . . . to have a sense of self . . . only rhetorical (not real)' (pp. 3–4).

Rom Harré draws on the work of pioneering Russian developmental psychologist Lev Vygotsky (1978), whose observational work with children shows that cognitive processes, including the ability to think about our-self, are developed through our interactions with others. Our beliefs and ideas about ourselves are entirely social: everything occurs twice, first in inter-personal interactions and then in the individual's mind (p. 43).

Richard Kearney (1996) describes Paul Ricoeur's maxim: 'The shortest route from self to self is through the other . . . the self is never enough . . .' The self 'constantly seeks out signs and signals of meaning in the other' (p. 1). The stories we tell ourselves about ourselves are based on those that others tell about us.

Rather than the idea that there is just one 'self', Rom Harré (2008) has developed three aspects of the self:

Self 1 – me in space and time

Self 2 – stories others tell about you

Self 3 – stories you tell about yourself

At school Barbara had developed a 'flippant', fun-loving 'self', which she later wanted to change; perhaps she wanted to alter stories told by teachers, friends and her parents? Perhaps she wanted to succeed at University, to follow her family's values of success through hard work? At university she had tried to create a different self, but her attempts to become less self-conscious had created a 'problematic' self.

The two older students she had made friends with were often too busy to talk on the phone or meet her. How were these voices influencing Barbara's self-descriptions? When her two friends were unavailable maybe she had seen this as a 'sign' that she was unpopular, or unable to make friends?

Perhaps she doubted her ability to make the 'friends for life' that she had dreamed of. I wondered if her 'flippant' self at school had got in the way of her studies. Perhaps this had led her to believe that she couldn't be successful in her academic work and also have friends.

Using these ideas I asked about the two older women. She said they were married with young children.

This gave me an idea. 'Doing a degree whilst being a young mother is pretty demanding,' I said, 'they may not have much time for phoning or meeting friends. But maybe they wish they had more time to meet you?' She nodded in agreement and confirmed that this was probably true.

'How would they describe their friendship with you if they were here?' I asked. She said that they would describe her as interesting and a good friend and they enjoyed being with her; the three of them swapped notes and helped each other prepare for essays. I hoped that bringing forth these voices (as in Rom Harré's Self 2, above) would help her tell different, more hopeful, stories about herself (as in Self 3) and that this would lead to her feeling better about her-'self'. We ended the conversation and Barbara told me that she would call me if she wanted to talk to me again.

A couple of months later at the beginning of the new academic year she asked to see me again. She wanted to ask my opinion about something and told me that everything was 'much better', that she was looking forward to the new academic year. And she thanked me for helping her.

Reflexive questions

Reflecting on a recent conversation with a client:

- Which grand narratives and presuppositions were influencing the conversation?
- Which 'Big' professional stories were influencing you?
- Which of your own personal stories were you connecting to?
- Which of these were useful to the client?
- Did the client's responses make you question any of these?
- Did you notice the ways in which the client had already started to change before coming to see you?
- Which of the client's skills and abilities did you notice?

2
THE POWER OF EMOTIONS

Why should therapists be interested in our emotions? After all, we are in service to the person who has sought our help; surely *clients'* feelings and emotions should be in the foreground, not ours? The image of the serene, impassive therapist unaffected emotionally by their clients is seductive. But this is a myth; practitioners do feel strong emotions about clients, and emotions are invaluable to self-reflexive practices.

Emotions involve bodily sensations, thoughts and cultural displays and are expressed and co-created through language (Rom Harré and Grant Gillett 1994). They are communications to other people and also to oneself. The emotions we feel involve moral judgements and are expressions of the choices we are making (Elsbeth McAdam and Peter Lang 2006). Indeed, all emotions are expressions of moral judgement, they say (p. 84).

If we feel bored, irritated or joyful we will express these feelings in subtle, or less than subtle, ways, which the client will pick up. Therapists' emotions have profound implications for the therapy and how clients come to feel about themselves. And they can affect the relationships clients have with other people in their life. For example, if I feel protective towards a client who is in an abusive relationship and angry on their behalf this may prevent me from exploring the 'logic' of these communications in the relationship and, more importantly, stop me from exploring less obvious ways in which the client is challenging the abuse. A therapist who 'knows' what is happening in the client's life has lost their 'curiosity', their deep respect for the whole system in which the client lives (Cecchin 1987).

Our emotions give us clues about our presuppositions, professional narratives and the personal stories that we are connecting with, and if we notice when we feel certain emotions this can help us question these prejudices.

Emotions give life its urgency (Keith Oatley 2004); they can be useful in alerting us to something important that the client is communicating, which we might otherwise have missed, providing both a connection with them and an opening to explore their stories.

Research shows that the emotion of hope is significant in successful therapeutic outcome (Jerome Frank and Julia Frank 1991). So, rather than viewing our emotions as a hindrance we can embrace them as an important resource. As Mony Elkaim (1990), says, 'The first tool of therapy is the therapist's own self. The feelings that arise in any member of a therapeutic system . . . mark the specific bridges that are being built between the . . . [client] and the therapist' (p. 163). Of course, each therapist has to decide the style of emotional connectedness that suits them and, most importantly, which style suits the client.

In the two years that I worked with Cecilie (pronounced Cecilia, her real name) I experienced a proverbial 'roller-coaster' of emotions. Sometimes I talked openly with her about my emotional responses to what she was saying and doing and she said this helped her see me as more 'human'. It also helped her understand how she affected others. I have discussed all this with her since we stopped working together as therapist and client and she has given me full permission to write this account of our work.

Emotions are communications

All the emotions I experienced during those two years were useful: my deep concern when she steadfastly refused to eat and I felt hopeless, despairing and frightened oriented me to what Cecilie herself could be living through. I found it extremely useful to search for respectful ways to check out with her what she was communicating emotionally and what these emotions were telling us.

I first met Cecilie when Jill, a nurse at the Student Medical Centre, rang to ask me to see a student who, she said, needed an appointment that day. I was fully booked and when our receptionist gave me the message I experienced, amongst other things, tenseness in my jaw and an agitation in my chest and stomach. The emotions in my body felt like an 'alarm call', they made me take notice.

The idea that emotions have central importance in our life is fairly recent. Charles Darwin (1872) didn't think emotions were of any use to adults, and the early psychologist William James (1884) thought that emotions had no influence on behaviour because they arose from behaviour. However, Rom Harré (2008; Rom Harré and W. Gerrod Parrott 1996), a professor of philosophy, says that emotions are *the* most important part of the everyday life of a human as well as being among the most complex (2008). As pragmatist philosopher John Dewey (1934) says, 'A lifetime would be too short to reproduce in words a single emotion' (p. 70).

Communications theorists argue that emotions are not a luxury: they are necessary and serve important functions in our social life (Rom Harré and W. Gerrod Parrott 1996). Emotions move us bodily; our heart may thump wildly, our stomach may appear to lurch and turn over, we may shake, tremble and sweat.

They are communications to the self; they give meaning to what is going on (Keith Oatley 1996: p. 312). They alert us to something important that needs our attention; however, like an alarm that shrills when there is a fire, an emotion doesn't actually show us what needs attention, just that something does. Emotions have a 'compulsive effect on us' (Mark Solms and Oliver Turnbull 2002). 'We cannot just lie back and feel our emotions. They make us want to do something' (p. 111). Biologically, emotions have invaluable functions; they prepare us for certain kinds of action (James Griffith and Melissa Elliott Griffith 1994).

Rom Harré identifies three broad areas in understanding how emotions operate; there is a:

(1) causal **bodily** component;
(2) **cognitive discursive** aspect – we make 'judgements' and evaluations, linked to our 'storyline';
(3) **social/cultural** display.

Inwardly emotions involve a release of hormones, changes in blood supply, heart rate, breathing and so on. Outwardly there are changes in facial expressions and complex behaviours like shouting, running away, and lashing out. We don't only experience our emotions, we also express them: some emotions, like fear, for example, involve both *perception* (the feeling of a racing pulse) and *action* (the urge to run or hide).

When a person describes a bodily experience as an emotion they are making some kind of judgement and evaluation. When we foreground a particular emotion, says Peter Lang (2008), this is an expression of our values; thus emotions are always a reflection of our morals. The judgements a person makes when they describe an emotion to themselves can be understood in cognitive and social terms and are often expressed in relation to what is important to them, their plans, goals and aspirations, and 'storyline'. It is because emotions arise from judgements that they can have moral relevance. They have personal *and* social functions and are communications to the self and to others (Oatley 1996: p. 312). Emotions, Glenda Fredman (2004) says, are created relationally and are always co-created with others, even if the other person is not physically there.

When Jill asked for an urgent appointment for her patient I first experienced a tenseness and physical agitation in my body. I tried to make sense of these bodily changes. Did they 'mean' apprehension, anticipation, anxiety, irritation, resentment and/or excitement? At that time I described my bodily sensations as a combination of irritation (with Jill), alarm and anxiety; I wanted to help a person in distress, but my timetable was packed. Other moral judgements swiftly followed: Jill had assumed that I had space in my diary to see a new client. At the same time I connected to a familiar personal and professional story, shared by many in our culture, that I want to be seen as hard-working. My storyline involved wanting to be known as a cooperative professional. My emotions were useful; they made me spring into action: I looked in my diary and saw that with some juggling I could offer Cecilie an appointment later that afternoon.

The language and 'rules' of doing an emotion

The best way to understand an emotion in any culture is to explore the rules in the specific vocabulary that is used in that culture to describe them (Harré 2008). In our culture emotions are often described as a kind of force or energy that motivates behaviour; anger, for example, is sometimes described like a coiled spring or the build-up of steam in a pressure valve (Lakoff and Kovecses 1983). Noticing the metaphors that are used when people talk about certain emotions can help us understand how they are used in that particular culture.

Every society and culture permits certain emotional displays and prohibits others. For example, the appropriate behaviour for 'doing' anger in our culture is to shout, scream and break things and involves the idea that one has been wronged (Averill 1982). However, there are always historical and cultural differences; for example, grief, which is seen as a basic, universal reaction to loss, varies between individuals and across cultures and has changed dramatically (Peter Stearns and Mark Knapp 1996: pp. 132–3). Some cultures react to grief with anger and seek vengeance or combat; some do not explicitly recognise grief. The Victorian way of mourning is now seen as 'excessive and unproductive . . . Grief . . . has undergone some surprisingly sharp turns over the past 150 years, and current reactions inevitably mirror this historical pathway' (p. 149).

Emotions are engendered (Catherine Lutz 1996). In our culture emotions are linked to the female and described as natural, irrational, chaotic, subjective, physical, unintended, as a sign of a character defect, and as a physical force and therefore dangerous; we view emotions as 'wild and unruly, a threat to order' and talk about someone controlling, coping with or managing their emotions (pp. 151–3); a 'rhetoric of control' is pervasive in the language of emotions (Michelle Rosaldo 1977).

I preferred not to discuss my emotional responses with Jill; the emotional 'rules' of the context did not permit my expressing them. Was it that I wanted to be seen as being 'in control' of my emotions? I could have shown my emotional response to another therapist as I was 'permitted' to do in these relationships but no-one was available so I talked to Marianne, our administrative secretary, who understood the organisational pressures. My emotions were a communication to myself and a communication to Marianne about the effect of this 'demand' on me.

Cultural displays and storylines

A neglected aspect of emotions that is now coming to the fore is the idea that they involve cultural and social displays; displays of emotions arise from within particular historical and social conditions and give us our cultural repertoire of emotions (Harré 2008). Some emotions are permitted within a particular context and some are forbidden. Which emotions a person is permitted to 'do' depends on the rights and duties in that particular context. In Western cultures certain emotional displays are sanctioned or forbidden in some work contexts: on television we have seen some male chefs shout and swear angrily at underlings in their kitchens and they consider that they have the 'right' to do so. It would be unusual for a top chef to be filmed crying, although in some work contexts people have the 'right' to cry. *How* a person expresses an emotion involves both a display and a 'storyline'.

My relationship with Jill and our two services was good and I wanted to be cooperative. I decided that it would not be helpful to our relationship or her view of me to make an emotional display of annoyance. This came from one of my professional (and personal) storylines: that I have chosen my profession in order to be helpful to others. Although I made the judgement that Jill's 'demand' for an 'urgent' appointment for her patient that day was not

34

necessary since I knew Cecilie was already seeing other professionals and was not suicidal, I wanted to help someone in distress. And I wanted to continue my good working relationship with Jill. All these storylines contributed to the emotions I 'noticed' and expressed.

Reflecting on our emotional posture

Working under pressure often makes therapists reach for familiar emotional responses. Taking time to notice one's emotional posture before meeting a client or family can help one take a reflexive position and, if necessary, this can help us alter our emotional stance. Glenda Fredman (2004), in her beautifully self-reflexive book *Transforming Emotions*, describes how, in preparing to meet a family, she realised that although she was looking forward to meeting them, she had become increasingly antagonistic towards the person who had referred the family.

She draws on James Griffith and Melissa Elliott Griffith's (1994) two emotional postures:

- tranquillity
- mobilisation

In a posture of 'tranquillity' we reflect, listen, wonder and muse, and so on. In a posture of mobilisation we want to act, and do something; we use justifying, scorning, shaming, controlling, distancing, protesting and defending language (p. 67).

In the pre-session conversation with her colleagues Glenda invited them to help her shift her emotional posture. Using a reflecting team approach (Tom Andersen 1990), they posed tentative, appreciative questions and offered multiple perspectives.

Therapists working alone without colleagues can adapt these questions to help us reflect on our emotional posture before meeting a client: We can ask ourselves:

- 'What emotional postures am I adopting right now?'
- 'Are these my preferred postures?'
- 'What postures do I want to create?'
- 'How might my posture affect the positions I can or can't take in the session?'
- 'If I could adopt a different posture, what might I do?'
- 'What can help me create opportunities for taking alternative positions?' (Fredman 2004: p. 84).

Although talking to Marianne was helpful, I would have valued a conversation with another therapist or a therapeutic team to help me reflect on my emotional posture towards Jill. My bodily sensations led me to make a judgement that I was feeling 'anxious' and 'irritated' and must respond right away, but, I reflected, this wasn't my preferred posture. So how could I shift it?

I wanted to be open to Cecilie when we met, without any residual annoyance towards Jill which could affect our conversation: if I thought Jill had created a drama where there was none, I might have ignored some very real concerns about Cecilie's well-being. On the other hand, if I were unduly anxious this could make me focus on 'risk factors' and possibly exclude other aspects of her story.

I reflected that practitioners from different disciplines have different demands and time-scales, which can lead to misunderstandings between them. I recalled what I knew about Jill's working context; she would spend ten minutes with a patient, whereas my first conversation with a new client takes an hour and a half. I would also need further time to write notes. Jill, and other members of staff, might not appreciate this.

I also thought about her professional storyline; she was, like me, a caring, responsible professional who wanted the best for her patients. She wanted them to get appropriate help as quickly as possible and she worked in a time-pressured context. I knew that when she made requests to other professionals they didn't always respond quickly. Also she worked in a blaming culture. Sometimes she expressed all this in a rather brusque way. Reflecting on this helped me take a posture of 'tranquillity' rather than one of 'mobilisation'.

Reflecting on other practitioners' different abilities, codes of conduct, organisational stresses and so on gives us information about how they respond emotionally to clients.

A recent conversation I'd had with Penny, another nurse, helped me reflect on Jill's communication style. Penny, who was new to the Student Medical Centre, asked me to help her develop her listening skills. She told me that she'd felt out of her depth when a student had begun talking about problems with her boyfriend.

I suggested that we re-play the conversation, with me being the patient. As I began talking (as the patient) I noticed an interested smile on her face; her eyes were bright and she nodded in a warm and caring way. But there was something amiss, something I couldn't quite put my finger on, that made me feel uneasy.

Afterwards, when we were discussing what she was feeling, I was surprised that in her inner talk Penny was saying, 'Oh, no! What on earth can I do to help?'

Penny's emotional reactions were signals to herself. She wasn't sure how to respond to the student. She had felt out of her depth, was starting to panic and wanted to run away. She wished she could have known what to say, to help the patient more. Although Penny appeared on the surface to be interested and caring, I had noticed something at a subtle level that wasn't quite right. Perhaps her smile and posture were a little static? Maybe Penny's anxiety made her forget to use her normal empathic responses? Her emotions of fear and panic had created a readying of her body to flee and this emotional posture had a subtle, but a very real, effect on me (as the patient).

This short conversation reminded me that practitioners with other kinds of training often feel emotionally overwhelmed when a person expresses complex emotional issues. It helped me to shift my position towards Jill. I could now focus my attention on the forthcoming meeting with Cecilie.

'Studying' emotions

The study of emotions crosses many disciplines and there is an exciting and growing rapprochement between neuroscience and psychotherapy (Antonio Damascio 2006; Jenny Corrigall and Heward Wilkinson 2003). Emotions are difficult to study and earlier 'reductionist' attempts to identify emotions through testing a person's adrenalin, for example, were not successful, Rom Harré (2008) says, because emotions are fleeting. The familiar idea of 'fight or flight' hormones kicking in when we sense danger is more complicated because these reactions can be simulated in the brain. There is no direct correlation between one's bodily state and an emotion: there is always a process of interpretation when we feel something in our body, which we then name as a particular emotion based on cultural stories. For example, he says that many bodily states, such as indigestion and wanting to go to the loo, are not considered to be emotions.

There are direct and complex interrelationships between the body, the brain, and our emotions, neuroscientist and psychologist Antonio Damascio (2006) says. Emotions are rational aspects of being human and 'are not the intangible and vaporous qualities that many presume them to be' (p. 164).

The body and the brain are important to our emotional reactions in the same way as in vision or speech (p. 131).

Stories we tell about ourselves

In between doing numerous other tasks throughout the day I identified a fluttery sensation in my stomach; what did this mean? As I prepared to meet Cecilie I scanned the information I had about her. Cecilie had come from Norway to London four years before. She was a dance student who had been at the university for four years, still in her second year of the three-year degree because she'd had several hospital admissions because of her complex relationship to food and eating. Not eating had affected her whole life, and her bmi (body mass index) was very low.

I had also heard that Cecilie had been sexually abused throughout her childhood and adolescence. Whilst many dance students focus on their body and have a fascination and an obsession with being thin, I guessed that Cecilie's past experiences were involved in her complex relationship with her body. In itself a dance degree is physically demanding; not eating must make this even harder.

She'd had at least ten continuous years of individual and family therapy in this country and in Norway, where she still had a therapist. And she was currently seeing eating disorder specialists as well as the senior GP and the senior nurse at the Student Medical Centre. As well as starving herself Cecilie was making herself sick, she had cut herself and had taken many overdoses. I felt a sense of 'alarm' as I reflected on this information. I reflected on my emotional posture: I felt metaphorically intimidated by all the practitioners and experts she had seen, and was seeing. In my self-talk I asked myself, 'What on earth can I offer her?'

A banal, yet extremely important aspect of being human is self-consciousness, says Rom Harré (2008). This neglected feature in our lives means that everyone is in a continual process of self-assessment; the stories people tell themselves about themselves are intimately interrelated with their emotions. Since we are continually assessing our performance, we are always in a process of creating our autobiography and re-writing our stories about ourselves (Bakhtin 1986).

When I was preparing to meet Cecilie my emotions involved the self-assessment that since none of the 'experts' had been able to help her, neither would I.

A gracious invitation

'When we meet a person,' says Peter Lang (2008), 'they are giving us a gracious invitation to be with them.'

Beginnings are tremendously important. We are creating situations in which people get connected. What gets co-created between us in those first moments? What happens in those beginnings? What are we doing to grow the relationship and create dignity? When we first meet a person how do we approach them with true curiosity? How do we put ourselves into a position of being open to them, with awe and wonder? How do we meet them in a different way? How do we meet someone with the eyes and ears of wonder, with an emotion of love, surprise, peace, not knowing?

When the time for the appointment came I glimpsed in the waiting area a slight, young woman. She looked much younger than her twenty-seven years; an elfin face, dark straight hair in a fringe, dark-coloured, loose clothes, bangles and a crocheted shawl. I liked her 'arty' look. When I introduced myself to her she looked up with enormous eyes. What struck me about Cecilie's facial expression was her eager look. This surprised me. I must have had a prejudice that she would be cynical or at least mistrustful of yet another practitioner.

The face is extremely important in assessing the emotions of the other. Our gaze goes first to the face when we meet another person; scanning the eyes and mouth in detail, touching and moving each other with our facial expressions. What we show on our faces often makes us aware of what we need to notice (Fredman, 2004: p. 68).

Cecilie was giving me a 'gracious invitation' to be with her. I wondered what stories enabled her to be so open to me given the numerous first meetings she must have had. I smiled, introduced myself, and led the way into the room. She gave a half-smile back as she got up to follow me. As we sat down together I felt honoured that she was willing to talk with me.

I thanked her for keeping the appointment and said I was delighted to meet her. Because Cecilie had not made the appointment herself, I wasn't sure whether she actually wanted to talk with me. But, as I noticed her willingness to engage with me, I felt more hopeful.

I showed her the specially-designed 'Introductory Consultation' pro-forma and explained that we would complete it together.

This approach to doing an Intake interview, in which therapist and client jointly co-create notes, uses appreciative, future-oriented questions. The therapist negotiates what the client wants written down and draws a genogram with them. After the first meeting the therapist writes an appreciative 'systemic story' or overview, which the client is invited to alter after it has been typed. The client is thus invited into a reflexive process (Fran Hedges 2000).

As I took the practical details of date, birth, address and so on I noticed an intense weariness in her posture. Perhaps the mere fact of having to give these details, yet again, was irksome. I decided to put the form to one side, explaining that we could complete it another time. Cecilie nodded and again gave me that half-smile.

'What are you hoping for from a conversation with me today?' I asked.

'I'm not sure,' Cecilie replied. She seemed exhausted. No wonder, I thought: attending dance classes whilst not eating would be affecting her physically and emotionally.

She sighed, adding, 'I just want to feel better.'

I accepted this as a 'gracious invitation' to join her in a conversation and said, 'I don't want you to feel you have to talk to me about anything you don't want to. Or go into things you've already gone into.' I felt great tenderness towards her and didn't want to hurt her. I wanted our first meeting to be a good one, to show her that I was open to her, as one human being meeting another. When I smiled she held my gaze with a penetrating look.

I was still thinking, she'll have talked endlessly about food, weight, not eating and the distressing issues in her past. I didn't want to repeat the kinds of conversations that hadn't helped her.

'You don't have to tell your story all over again . . . unless you want to . . .' I said. Cecilie gazed back at me and I felt an emotion of love beginning to flow between us. I was still wondering what on earth I could do that would be sufficiently different and useful for this young woman who had talked with so many people.

I noticed her body posture as she began to relax in the chair. At least we seemed to be making a good connection. Maybe my 'tranquil', yet alert body posture and the way I had abandoned the Introductory Consultation form enabled her to feel my appreciative emotions of love, awe and wonder as we talked together?

Opening pathways to more hopeful futures

Exploring a person's future hopes and dreams can help therapists notice what is getting in the way of more hopeful emotions. As Peter Lang (in McAdam and Lang 2009) puts it so elegantly, 'Problems are frustrated hopes and dreams.'

An idea began to form: I guessed that many other therapists had worked with Cecilie around food, eating and weight. Had they, I wondered, explored her hopes and dreams for the future? I wondered what could be blocking her pathways to more hopeful futures? At the time, I felt that there was nothing else I could offer.

'I'm wondering about your hopes for the future,' I began in a tentative preamble, watching her closely. She seemed to be listening intently.

'What kinds of wishes, dreams and visions do you have?' I went on. 'What kinds of things would you like to do in the future?'

I was expecting her to talk about a future in dance; after all, she had sacrificed a great deal just to stay on the course. To my utter amazement she said she wanted to become a journalist. I felt excited by this unexpected information. For someone who had difficulties with food and body image this career path could, I thought, be a healthier option.

I felt a flicker of something in the area of my chest, a small vibration that felt like hope. I allowed my emotions of wonder, awe and excitement to show in my face, voice and body as I asked what she enjoyed about writing, what was attractive about the idea of doing this work and what kind of journalist she would like to be.

Cecilie became more animated, fixing me with her gigantic eyes as she talked excitedly about loving the process of writing and wanting to help others to understand about the effects of 'eating disorders' (her words). Tiredness seemed to leave her face and body.

Hope and hopelessness

I sensed something igniting between us. This spark of hope eclipsed my earlier doubts. And in that moment I recollected conversations I'd had with other people who had complex relationships with food and their bodies, recalling that they'd found it useful to talk with me.

Hope is tremendously important in doing effective psychotherapy (Snyder et al. 1999). A hopeful practitioner is crucial in overcoming demoralisation; and clients must sense that they have helped others reach their goals (Frank and Frank 1991). Conversely, 'Hopelessness', Kaethe Weingarten (2007) says, induces therapists 'to ask questions that worsen the problem' and they lack the complexity to create new, and more hopeful, ideas (p. 18). However, hope needs 'anchoring in practice' (Paulo Freire 1992). 'The naïve idea that hope alone will transform the world is an excellent route to hopelessness . . . hope needs practice in order to become historical concreteness' (pp. 8–9).

There are two main ways of 'doing hope':

(a) 'agency thinking': 'I can do it';
(b) 'pathways thinking': 'Here's how I can do it.'

Helping people to identify their abilities and setting goals activates the reward circuitry of the prefrontal cortex; helping people to devise pathways toward their goals, 'doing hope . . . activates a neurochemical cascade that dampens fear and makes people feel more hopeful' (Richard J. Davidson 2003).

It was fortunate that I genuinely appreciated Cecilie's love of words and writing. Yet, if she had said she wanted to be a lawyer or a dog trainer I would also have wanted to explore these dreams.

Now I asked Cecilie what she was doing about these hopes and dreams, in other words, was there any reality to them?

She told me that there was a module in dance journalism, which would combine her love of dance with her love of writing. It seemed that she believed she could do it, and there was also 'a pathway' to her dream.

As Rom Harré (in Harré and Parrott 1996) shows, the metaphors and vocabulary we use when we describe an emotion help us understand how it works within a particular culture. For example, hope in our culture, James Averill (1996) says, is described as something a person *has*, something that can be lost or found, given or received, shattered or restored, rather than what a person *does*, although hope may also spur a person to action. We often talk about hope being an energy that may fill us until we burst. However, the 'energy' of hope is more like that found in food, nourishing, sustaining and supporting us when no action is possible (p. 29). In Western history hope has been seen as a central emotion, although some consider it to be a cognitive or 'intellectual' emotion because there is little bodily involvement. 'Hope is less tangible, less demonstrable, more open-ended than anger or love . . . it is more like a dream, fantasy, or illusion' (pp. 25–7).

Like all emotions, hope is not universal; it varies between cultures; in the course of James Averill's (1996) research, 'hope' was mentioned in America, Australia, Puerto Rico and Japan, whereas in Korea, Indonesia, Malaysia and Sri Lanka hope was not mentioned as an important emotion. The philosophical and religious differences between Koreans and Americans subtly influence their attitudes towards hope, he says. Americans are influenced by the Judeo-Christian tradition where hope has been highly prized as an emotional state: hope, faith and charity being the three 'theological virtues'. Conversely, Koreans, influenced by Confucianism, Buddhism and Taoism, strive to become morally perfect (pp. 35–6).

As we talked I noticed Cecilie talking more quickly and in a more animated way and felt a tremendous 'surge' of hopefulness. We were both nourished and sustained by our mutually spiralling language of hope.

Noticing and encouraging resilience

During the conversation Cecilie began talking about feeling exhausted because of difficulty with sleeping at night. She often missed her classes because she had to catch up on her sleep during the daytime: a vicious circle.

'What do you do when you're awake in the night?' I asked.

She said she'd got up at 3.00 a.m. that morning. Her tone was hesitant and I sensed that she was trying to decide whether to tell me something. Eventually she 'confessed' that she had walked round the campus and had ended up at the Security Officers' Gate House. She said one of the security officers had been kind and talked to her; after a while she'd felt better and had gone back to bed and managed to get some sleep.

I applauded her resourcefulness and ability to seek help from an appropriate and caring person (security officers are in positions of trust).

'What did you do that encouraged him to help you?' I asked. She seemed unable to answer so after a few moments I said, 'You seem to draw people towards you; so many people want to help you. What is it that you do that invites people to be kind, and go out of their way for you?' I was noticing the way she was inviting me to help her and over time I learned about countless others who went out of their way to do things for her.

She found these questions difficult to answer at the time; yet, as she told me later, they resonated for her. She said that she'd expected me to criticise her for this 'risky behaviour' and was surprised and pleased with this new angle.

D. S. Charney's (2004) review of the psychobiology of resilience and vulnerability notes that 'resilient people may have "a reward system that is . . . hypersensitive to reward . . . despite chronic exposure to neglect and abuse"' (Charney 2004: p. 205, cited in Weingarten 2007: p. 21):

> in resilient individuals, the neural networks associated with social coop-eration and mutual altruism may be more densely linked to reward centres in the brain . . . making bonding and attachment to others more gratifying. (Weingarten 2007: p. 21)

I recalled that Jill, the nurse, had 'demanded' that I see Cecilie 'urgently'; the security officer had been kind to her. Although practitioners had described Cecilie as an unfortunate victim of sex abuse with a life-threatening eating disorder, my emotions helped me to pay attention to her extraordinary resilience and ability to attract help.

I began meeting Cecilie regularly. Her resilience showed in her enormous range of creative responses to harrowing life events: drawings, paintings and writing, some done as an in-patient; photography and inventive knit-ting. She showed me pictures of her family and friends. And we drew 'future dream maps' and friendship charts. Once, at the end of the conversation, she asked for a hug, and this became an ending ritual that she said helped to sustain her through challenging times.

A response, an invitation and a response

Cecilie only ate tiny amounts of food at the best of times; then during the autumn term I realised that she had actually stopped eating. Although she obviously enjoyed our conversations, which eventually involved spirited discussions about food and body image, they made no difference to her eating behaviour; she was adamant that she was not going to eat. I felt frightened and frustrated. What if she did actually die? 'It's your choice whether you kill yourself through not eating,' I once said, 'although I would be devastated if you died. I'm not going to persuade you to do what you don't want to do. So many people have been trying for so long to force you to eat and I don't want to do the same.'

44

'We have to find some way to manage our anxiety so as not to burden the client with it,' my supervisor Peter Lang said. 'When people come to see us they have to have some hope that we will help them.' None the less, when we pick up anxiety this is an invitation to respond, to take the client's position seriously.

Although nothing was changing as far as her eating was concerned I continued to admire Cecilie's resilience and creativity and we found ways to keep her dreams alive, one of which was our mantra: 'We'll show 'em.' However, the medics were worried; when the doctor said, 'We have to accept that she might die,' I felt intense fear and anxiety. From their position the therapeutic work was not 'working'.

Amazingly she continued to attend dance classes and lectures, although she sometimes didn't have enough energy to get out of bed. When she starved herself, Cecilie said, she enjoyed the feeling of weakness, emptiness and an emotion of triumph over her body; a 'skill' she had developed from an early age.

The paradox was that in spite of doing everything to put her life in jeopardy, she didn't seem to believe that she would die. Although I felt intense anxiety about her well-being, I would say, 'There's some logic to your not eating, but we don't understand it – yet . . .'

Patterns that connect

Using Gregory Bateson's (1972; 1979) ideas of pattern and interconnectedness, the Milan team developed the 'logical' or 'positive connotation' showing that if we focus on only one part of 'the system', such as what one person is doing, their behaviour may seem inexplicable, but when we widen the context to include other relevant people and social or cultural stories this new information can give us new understandings of the meanings people give for their actions. And if we describe people as doing the best they can, given all the circumstances, this opens us up to different stories (Lynn Hoffman 1992; Selvini Palazzoli et al. 1978; 1980).

I kept wondering: What was keeping these stories alive and to whom were these emotions a communication (apart from the professionals)?

Cecilie's mother first noticed the pattern that helped me make sense of what she was communicating. When she was at home with her in Norway Cecilie would eat, albeit it with difficulty; when she returned to London she would starve herself.

What was this pattern of emotions communicating, and to whom, I asked myself.

My emotions were alerting me to something serious; the moral position I took made me consider that my fear and anxiety were responses to Cecilie's invitation: she was inviting me to keep her alive and protect her from harm. The pattern her mother had noticed provided an important clue to the 'logic' of Cecilie's puzzling behaviour. And then, although in retrospect this seems obvious, I began to wonder whether these emotions were, amongst other things, important communications about the complex relationship she had with her mother.

After many invitations, a year and a half after my first meeting with Cecilie her mother agreed to join us when she came to London. When she arrived I thanked her for her 'gracious invitation' to allow me to be part of their conversation. We had a long, passionate discussion about many aspects of their relationship, which was deeply moving for all of us.

Cecilie saw this conversation as a turning point and the beginning of a stronger relationship with her mother. And when she was offered a place on an intensive, ground-breaking programme in Norway for people with long-term eating difficulties she accepted it. This meant leaving university and her friends in London, which was a great wrench. This signalled a new phase in her relationship with her mother and her view of herself and the future.

Review

A year later when Cecilie came to London on a visit, my colleague Heleni Andreadi and I interviewed her. She remembered the first meeting she'd had with me. It was different from those she'd had with other practitioners, she said.

'What was different about it?' Heleni asked. Turning to me, Cecilie said, 'You were the only person who talked to me like I was a whole person.'

'How did she do this?' Heleni asked.

'She didn't focus on my problems,' Cecilie replied. 'She didn't focus on food or eating or my weight like everybody else did. She was interested in me; she asked me what I was interested in.'

Later she said that my appreciative approach enabled her to participate in the eating disorder programme in Norway.

'I couldn't have done it without you,' she said many times. 'You helped me believe I was a worthwhile person.' I felt great joy at hearing those words.

Epilogue

Cecilie engaged in what turned out to be a challenging behavioural programme in a Norwegian hospital over the following two years and she still receives support from these therapists. Her relationship with her mother and other members of her family is a source of joy and strength. She is completing a teacher training course, which she loves and obviously excels at. She has a part-time job and is buying her own flat. Her weight is 'normal' and she has a 'normal' relationship with food.

When she came to visit me a year later we fulfilled one of the dreams that had sustained us: we had a three-course lunch in a smart restaurant and she took a photo of herself eating Eton Mess (strawberries, meringues and cream).

I am hugely appreciative of the 'gracious invitation' Cecilie gave me to accompany her on that two-year emotional voyage. I want to extend my appreciation to her mother for agreeing to talk with me and for never ceasing to support her.

Reflexive questions

Thinking about a client with whom you have worked:

- Describe your emotional posture before, during and after your conversations.
- How did your storylines, language, bodily feelings influence your actions (your 'display')?
- How did your ethical and moral stance affect your relationship with them?
- If we asked the client, would they say that your emotions were helpful, or not?
- Did you alter your self-assessments and autobiography in any way?

3

HOW LANGUAGE AFFECTS OUR ASSUMPTIONS AND PREJUDICES

When I was growing up my mother used to say, 'Sticks and stones will break my bones, but words will never hurt me.' It was her way of telling me not to get upset when other children called me names.

But words *can* hurt us; language is powerful and has the ability to energise, wound and thrill us. Words are speaking deeds, John Shotter (2004) says; actions, and certain words, have the power to 'move' or 'strike' us and draw our attention to unique details of people's lives that might otherwise have passed both of us unnoticed.

Communication is the stuff of therapy and all aspects of language are our tools and have enormous power to co-create the worlds in which we and our clients live. Reflexive therapists constantly think about how we are affecting the people who come to talk with us. Using a broader view of language, we communicate in diverse ways through our tone of voice, gestures, what we wear, what our bodies are saying, what we put in our letters and reports, and through the architecture, layout and visual images in our therapy spaces, as well as with the words we use.

It is important for therapists to understand that although we may have good intentions we cannot know the possible effect that we could be having on clients by what we say, how we say it and all the other ways that we are communicating. Language is not a neutral instrument, says communications professor Barnett Pearce (2007). It is *the* primary way in which we co-create our social worlds, shape our lives, co-create meaning and constitute ourselves (p. 201). It is 'the single most powerful tool that humans have ever invented for the creation of social worlds' (Pearce 1994: p. 71).

Language not only *reveals* our assumptions, perceptions and values but *creates* them. Through language we literally participate, create and live in the worlds we create (Vernon Cronen and Peter Lang 1994).

We are born into language and inherit all that comes with it: history, culture, tradition, and so on. Language is . . . the vehicle through which we ascribe meaning, make sense of our lives, give order to our world, and relate our stories. We act and react through language, using it to relate, to influence, and to change. (Harlene Anderson 1997: p. 204)

How many experts are aware of how their expert-language bewitches them and produces their prejudices? asks Tom Andersen (1998), following the revolutionary work of Ludwig Wittgenstein (1953). We can't escape from this bewitchment of language. 'One might say that part of being a person is to be bewitched and to be prejudiced. We can neither *not* be bewitched nor not prejudiced . . . it is *the big assumption* . . . ' (p. 79).

When we talk with clients this is a messier and more ambiguous process than any written account can show. As Walter Ong (1982) puts it so eloquently, 'Like butterflies in a museum, words in print are killed, impaled, and held up for display in an artificial setting' (p. 74). With this in mind, the following discussion shows how reflexive conversations with a client helped us resolve a misunderstanding.

When Lottie, a black British woman in her early forties, came to the University Counselling Service she told me she had been feeling unhappy for some time. I noted Lottie's use of the word 'unhappy'. Before asking her what she meant by this I asked what she wanted from our conversation and in her future. She told me that she wanted to feel better and that problems in a previous job still made her feel bad about herself.

The late lamented transmission model

A popular approach to verbal language is to describe it as an expression of our thoughts: we think something, and put that thought into words. The assumption that we put across what is in our 'mind' when we speak to another person has been critiqued. This 'late lamented transmission model', Barnett Pearce (1994) says, is as far from how we communicate as to be beyond all recognition (p. 20). Wittgenstein turned the earlier 'modernist' view upside down, showing that language is *the* most powerful, subtle and important tool or instrument that human beings use in order to think. There are no intrinsic meanings in language; as he shows, the meaning of a word is always in the way it is used in a context (Rom Harré and Michael Tissaw 2005: p. 172). It is a fundamental error, claims Wittgenstein, to have the idea that there are thoughts *as well as* the words that we use, although of course we do have other tools, such as images, feelings, non-verbal symbols, models, drawings and so on.

There are inherent contradictions, paradoxes, semantic clashes and linguistic traps whenever we talk about language. Because 'it is in language that we speak about language . . . language always speaks about itself' (Heinz von Foerster, Foreword in Elkaim 1990: p. xi). Wittgenstein wants us to be reflexively self-aware of our own use of words, his central achievement being a set of 'methods' for talking about our everyday talk, John Shotter (2005) says. One of Wittgenstein's methods is to remind us that in our conversations we continually point things out that would otherwise escape our notice. 'We are continually saying to each other, "Look at this!" (we point things out to each other); "Look at it *like* this" (change each other's perspective); "Think what you did last time" (remind each other)' and so on (Shotter 2005: p. 188).

The power of our metaphors

The metaphors we use when we talk are powerfully influential in focusing our attention, structuring our thoughts, and guiding our actions. Wittgenstein used copious metaphors throughout his writings to help him convey his complex ideas. Metaphor is not simply an aspect of language, but a primary form of cognition, enabling people to translate abstract ideas into words (George Lakoff and Mark Johnson 1999, cited in Hunt and Sampson 2006: p. 21).

It is not sufficiently acknowledged by practitioners that the language we use can highlight certain features about a person and obscure others. Indeed, Harlene Anderson (1997) maintains, those who train practitioners are not aware of the effect of their clinical language on the people who seek our help. James Griffith and Melissa Elliott Griffith (1994) write about how therapists' language reveals their prejudices. 'The psychoanalyst . . . [uses] language of wishes, fears, unconscious mind, and interpretations. The cognitive behaviourist meets the patient as a coach meets an athlete . . . using language of behavioral reinforcement . . . cognitive distortions . . . ' and so on (pp. 22–3).

Lottie told me she had worked in local government and was now doing a degree. When I used the phrase 'professional woman' she was surprised and pleased. I noted that by taking a drop in salary she was creating the possibility of a different, and better, future. She liked this language, which helped her co-create more positive descriptions about herself.

Nancy Boyd-Franklin (1989), in her key text on working therapeutically with black families, says that for complex historical reasons it often takes time for a black person to trust a therapist (black or white).

Every time she came to see me Lottie began to divulge more and more. After three meetings she told me about a 'shameful' time in the previous job when she was wrongly accused of professional negligence. I felt honoured that she had trusted me enough to talk about this and told her briefly of my non-white dual heritage and the effects of being an 'outsider' in this culture, and also something about my personal struggles in the workplace. This, she said, helped her trust me.

But, she said, it was as if a permanent cloud were hanging over her. She described with her hands a metaphorical shape floating above her head. I visualised a dark, heavy cloud hovering there, a metaphor that turned out to have tremendous power.

Lottie talked about her continuing feelings of shame and distress, illustrated by 'the cloud'. I said that I had set up a free homeopathic service with volunteer homeopaths, which many clients found helpful alongside therapy. And she eagerly agreed to book an appointment with one of the homeopaths.

After two more meetings with me and two meetings with Claire, the homeopath, Lottie said she was feeling much better and that the cloud had 'lifted'. I was thrilled and said so. Since she was feeling brighter she said she would call me if and when she needed to make another appointment. I honoured her decision to use conversations with me in this way, showing her that I supported her decision.

As we said goodbye I said she was welcome to make an appointment to see me at any time. My language, focus on her hopes for the future, spotting her determination and accepting that she knew best about when to seek therapy revealed my biases.

It might be more difficult to do this if there is a statutory responsibility to do therapy with a client or if a therapist is concerned about a client's welfare.

I saw Lottie about a month later when we bumped into each other just after her appointment with Claire, the homeopath. We greeted each other warmly and the three of us stood in the corridor for moment; Lottie laughed and thanked both of us, saying how much better she was feeling. There was an atmosphere of celebration. And, wanting to thank Claire for her work, I made an appreciative comment about the beneficial effects of homeopathy. It was 'a minor miracle', I said, that 'the cloud' had disappeared. Then we all went our separate ways. It had seemed a joyous occasion.

Three weeks later Lottie made an appointment to see me. I greeted her warmly. Right away she said she had been upset by what I had said. I was alarmed that I had inadvertently offended her and asked her to explain.

'I can't believe you said such an insensitive thing,' she said, 'especially since you seemed to understand how it feels to be a black woman. I've been wrestling with it for weeks.'

I was puzzled and dismayed. I only remembered the occasion as being celebratory; my recollection was of a light-hearted conversation that had acknowledged Claire's work, which was voluntary, and the positive effect of the homeopathic remedy.

'What did I say?' I asked.

'You said a black cloud had lifted,' she answered.

Understanding gradually began to dawn, as she continued, 'it's like you see a black woman and think black cloud.'

She didn't need to add that there was an implicit connection between an 'unwanted black cloud' and an 'unwanted black woman'.

The meaning of a word depends on its use

Although linguists once thought that there was an essential meaning for every word, this is a fundamental mistake; 'the meaning of a word is its use in the language' (Wittgenstein 1953: no. 43). Meanings emerge as we talk and act together; words have a 'pattern of uses', multiple meanings rather than having an essential or common meaning. The meaning of a word depends on the context in which it is used and the *way* we use it. 'Only in the stream of thought and life do words have meaning' (Ludwig Wittgenstein 1981: no. 173). 'When I think in language, there aren't "meanings" going through my mind in addition to the verbal expressions,' Wittgenstein says (1953), 'the language is itself the vehicle of thought' (no. 329).

The language a person uses, the word, or rather the 'utterance' – a 'unit of speech communication' which could be a word, phrase or even a gesture

– is never simply our own; it is always half of someone else's, says Mikhail Bakhtin (1981: p. 345). Most of us will never use a word that hasn't already been used by thousands of other people who did not mean what we mean by it. We can adopt creative approaches to words to suit us but we can never own them. Words are what Bakhtin (1986) calls 'interindividual'; the meanings of words do not exist *either* in a person's mind, *or* in the world around them, they are *created* between people; 'there is no such thing as a private language; language is public and relational' (p. 88).

Lottie was right; I had visualised the cloud she had described being above her head as heavy, dark and, yes, black. Lottie and I had different cultural references and different associations with the word 'black'. Mine included Dylan Thomas's use of the word in his poem Under Milk Wood: *'. . . bible-black . . . sloeblack, slow, black, crowblack . . .'. I also connected to the 'black is beautiful' movement, the many shades of black in dyes, paint, and clothing and 'the little black dress'. Lottie, on the other hand, had other associations; her personal, cultural and historical relationships with the word 'black' were different from mine.*

The issue of colour throws up complexities for all therapists, says Nancy Boyd-Franklin (1989). 'The mark of slavery has never fully disappeared for Black people . . . the feelings and assumptions that formed the psychological underpinnings of the slaveholding structure have yet to be purged from the national psyche' (p. 32).

She is writing about the American context but there are enough similarities to the British and European cultures to make her comments more widely relevant. The cultural references to the word 'black' include the iniquity of slavery and inequalities that black people still experience. 'All Black people,' Nancy Boyd-Franklin continues, 'irrespective of the color, shade, darkness, or lightness are aware from a very early age that their blackness makes them different from mainstream White [society].'

I was a therapist, who in multi-cultural London appeared to be white, talking with another professional who was clearly white with a client who was black, celebrating the disappearance of something unwanted, something 'black'. Lottie was a black British woman from an African-Caribbean heritage, living in twenty-first-century London.

I knew that Lottie was also making personal connections with the tough time she'd had in her previous job and the discrimination she had suffered there. Whilst my intention was to notice the positive changes in Lottie's life, compliment Claire and value homeopathic treatment, she had experienced our conversation as hurtful; what I had said seemed to disregard her history and her life experiences.

Words are polysemic; the same word might therefore carry very different meanings for different persons. Wittgenstein (1953: no. 12) uses the tool metaphor or analogy; 'he points out that words are like the handles in a locomotive cabin. They look "more or less alike," but their functions are different).' Today we might think of switches in the cockpit of a plane (Harré and Tissaw 2005: p. 74). Most of the time when we are asking about the meanings of words we are really asking about *uses*, the way we use words within a particular context. 'Wittgenstein's fundamental insight in the treatment of psychology is that language and the meaning of our words takes place in the conversations we have with others; specifically it is in their application, how we *use* words' (p. 67). Indeed, it is futile to seek the meaning of a word in some underlying intention or within the unconscious; the meanings of words develop within specific contexts in unfolding conversations and patterns of relationship.

I was shocked that I had not appreciated the meaning that Lottie would give to this particular word and that I had converted an unwanted aspect of her life, 'a heavy cloud', into 'a black cloud'. I understood that she saw this as an offensive description.

Lottie and I were in different socio-economic positions and different power positions: I was Lottie's therapist; she was telling me about her difficulties and was seeking help from me. Our different skin colour reinforced these historically-constituted, differential power positions. Lottie found it helpful that although, as I told her, I appeared to be white I had grown up in post-war rural Britain with my Palestinian mother, who was a lone parent in the days before this was considered normal.

Skin colour, Nancy Boyd-Franklin says, remains 'toxic' in many black families and provides 'fertile ground for the development of family myths and secrets . . . that are rarely discussed'. They include 'family secrets about birth, paternity, and informed adoption'. Children may be favoured or rejected because of lighter or darker skin colour (p. 38). In 'Black families . . . a child's skin color can help to explain why a child has been singled out for the family projection process and . . . targeted as the family scapegoat' (Boyd-Franklin 1989: pp. 34–5). As John Lanamann (1998) says, 'the embodied aspects of persons . . . especially . . . those . . . who do not have power and control have been rendered invisible' (p. 298).

Stories from my own family could have made me more sensitive: one of my cousins, growing up in Jordan within her own culture, had a negative self-identity because her skin colour was darker than that of her siblings. My mother was described as 'the black woman' and we were marked out as different in rural England.

In the spontaneity of that conversation with Lottie and Claire my family stories had not helped me to 'see' or 'hear' how the word 'black' used in this way would be hurtful to someone with Lottie's life history, cultural background and colour. In my adult life living in multi-cultural London, my skin colour goes unnoticed. I referenced the term 'black cloud' to my current stories and was 'colour blind' in this context. Lottie, who was a black woman with a dark skin colour, referenced the term to her life experiences and her own cultural and historical position.

Our trust had been tested, but that Lottie was willing to confront me and tell me about the effect on her of my language confirmed our strong relationship.

Speech acts

Any discussion of language must involve episodes of communication in which meanings are co-created, as well as how they emerge in our conversations. Episodes are, 'sequences of speech acts, punctuated with a beginning and an end, and united by a story' (Pearce 2007: p. 131). The smallest unit of communication is the 'speech act', which entails three conversational 'turns': the 'conversational triplet' (p. 117). A response can be to something that was said a long time ago and any response always has a consequence; even if we say nothing or walk away, this is still a *response* with a *consequence*. We never speak in a vacuum; whatever we say always exists as a *response* to things that have been said before and in anticipation of things that will be said in *response* (Bakhtin 1986: p. 126). This perfectly describes the conversational triplet.

Lev Vygotsky (1986), the innovative Russian psychologist, talks about the interactive nature of thought and language. Putting thoughts into words, he says, is a process. There is,

> a continual movement backward and forth from thought to word and from word to thought. . . . Thought is not merely expressed in words; it comes into existence through them.   (p. 255)

Every thought tends to connect something with something else, to establish a relation between things. Every thought moves, grows and develops, fulfils a function, solves a problem.   (p. 218)

To make things simple I am focusing on just this short episode within the one conversation. I describe the speech acts and the different 'turns' in the episode.

The first was when Lottie told me she was upset with me. This was not strictly-speaking the 'first' turn since Lottie was responding to all our previous conversations.

The second turn (in this episode) was my response to Lottie, listening to her and asking how I had upset her. At every point when I responded to what Lottie said there were many other things I could have said, and done; each would have invited a different response and had different consequences.

The third turn was when she told me I'd been insensitive.

The fourth turn was when I asked her to explain further.

The fifth turn was when she told me what I'd said.

Even though I was shocked, as Lottie was speaking I began to reflect on how to respond: should I explain my intentions or try to put things right? Both, I reflected, could shift the focus from Lottie's feelings onto mine, thus hi-jacking the conversation.

In the sixth turn, despite being mortified by my blunder, I thanked Lottie for her generosity in telling me how upset she had been, saying briefly that I had not meant to offend her and was sorry that I had been so oblivious to the meaning of that word.

My responses were useful: Lottie accepted my apology.

Endless re-descriptions of the world

At every 'turn' each of us could have used different language, which would have affected the other person's response and the conversation could have veered off into a different, and possibly less helpful, direction. Fortunately, as Mikhail Bakhtin (1986) says, we are engaged in a process of endless re-descriptions of the world. Because we act into situations that are unfinished and undetermined by our actions we usually have opportunities to change things.

In my inner talk I was thinking that it had taken many meetings for her to trust me; she'd said, 'You seem to understand what it's like being a black woman.' Maybe, because of my comment, Lottie had revised her wisdom in trusting me? Perhaps she had thought that it would have been easier for her not to have come to see me, never to have told me about the way my comment had affected her?

Lottie told me she had wrestled with the meaning of my comment. But because she had decided to tell me about her sense of betrayal this gave us the opportunity to co-create some new descriptions.

Lottie didn't know how I would respond but she was willing to talk to me and this created the possibility that we could explore the different meanings each of us had given for what I had said.

Moving from deficit to affirmative language

It is little wonder that most of us use negative language without realising it when research shows that 90 per cent of the comments made to children are negative (David Cooperrider, in Barnett Pearce 2007: p. 107).

I described Lottie to myself as being generous in giving me an opportunity to respond to her. She was, I thought, willing to take time out from her busy schedule. Maybe it had taken courage for her to come to talk to me. Perhaps this showed that she trusted me enough to speak about something so deeply sensitive. I didn't want to assume any of this, so decided to check my ideas out with her. Lottie said she was pleased by the way I explored these ideas with her as although she had trusted me, which had given her the courage to confront me, she wasn't sure of my response.

We have 'a moral responsibility . . . to co-create worlds that people want to live in . . . if we create negative worlds, we live in negative worlds'. The things we focus on create the lives people live. Exploring the 'hurt' and the 'problems' will constitute people's lives (Elsbeth McAdam and Peter Lang 2006: p. 87). For example, if Lang and McAdam are working with someone whose drinking creates a problem, instead of asking how they are going to be a 'non-drinking person', they can explore what they want to create and what they are going to do to create that. If you keep the negative words 'not drinking', you still have 'drinking' in focus. There is no clear visualisation of an alternative way to act. If there is a concern about a child in a family they will use the same principles in an 'above suspicion and beyond risk' interview. On the phone to the parents they will say, 'We know that, as good parents, you want to come and discuss this with us.' This brings forth the identity of *good* parents, of *caring* parents, of *loving* parents. At the meeting they will explore how the parents will ensure the *safety* of their child. To hear and agree, to 'witness' what has happened to a person is useful, but it is not enough. When there has been abuse, for example, witnessing alone does not create safety; the adults have to agree to behave in a way that is 'above suspicion' – people have to do something different to ensure that something different is created in the future (p. 102).

I didn't avoid talking about Lottie's painful time when she was accused of professional negligence but I combined this with a discussion of what she had done, and was doing, to create a different future.

Tone, gestures, clothes, touch and other non-verbal language

When we think about language we tend to think about the words we use, verbal language. But language is inseparable from the bodily act of 'speaking'. Wittgenstein (1981) refers to the strongly musical element in verbal language: a sigh, the intonation of a voice in a question, in an announcement, in longing, all the innumerable gestures made with the voice (no. 161). 'Language comprises all kinds of utterances . . . both words (sounds) and bodily activities; language is activities' (Andersen 1998: p. 75). Smiling, frowning, gestures and our posture, such as leaning back or leaning forwards, crossing or uncrossing our legs, shifting position at particular times during the conversation, are also powerful ways in which we 'speak'. There is no point trying to avoid these non-verbal cues, trying to be a 'blank screen'; whatever we say, or don't say, will communicate something; we cannot *not* communicate (Cecchin et al. 1994: p. 29).

Going 'beyond language both in our thinking and in our techniques', according to Rabia Malik and Inga-Britt Krause (2005), is important because 'bodies . . . are cultural and political'. What we wear, how we sit, stand and move, whether or not we touch are important (p. 106). Other aspects of 'non-verbal' language include symbols that indicate our social positioning, such as what we wear and what our clothes communicate. There are subtle non-verbal aspects of language in which members of a social community gesture to one another and social divisions become embodied. Social class, for example, is never eradicated when there has been a social revolution, Rom Harré (2008) says, because we cannot eradicate the subtle micro-communications and the myriad non-verbal ways in which we communicate.

My tone of voice and facial expressions as well as the appreciative words I used showed Lottie the admiration I felt for her. My gender, body shape and size, and skin colour were immediately apparent to her, as were my clothes, jewellery and so on. My race and ethnicity were less obvious. As noted, the differences in our skin colour gave particular meaning to my 'black cloud' comment. When Lottie told me how upset she'd been with me I conveyed my respect for what she was saying with an attentive body posture and eager tone of voice.

Lottie now said that she had a presentation to make and wanted to understand why she always doubted herself. She sat forward in the chair in what seemed to be a tense manner. We had explored her developing abilities and the theme of self-doubt before, and rather than reiterate these conversations I said that I also felt daunted in certain settings especially if I was about to embark on something new and challenging. She listened keenly then flung her arms up and said, 'No! Really? Do you?' As I grinned and nodded she went on, 'Even you, looking so stylish and professional?'

I enjoyed Lotte's statement, which I took to mean that she was surprised that someone she saw as being 'stylish and professional' could also, at times, feel daunted. As well as what I said verbally, the 'language' of my job title and my clothes 'spoke volumes'.

In reply I said that she looked pretty classy herself, with her avant-garde style. Lottie gave a sideways smile as she reflected for a moment. All of a sudden she leaned forward and said, 'Can I have a hug?' I was taken aback, yet felt honoured and readily agreed. We leaped up together, and hugged each other enthusiastically.

How comfortable are we with touch and other non-verbal expressive language? It is important for each of us to acknowledge our preferred style and some therapists would not be comfortable with this type of bodily contact. At the same time, Jim Wilson (2007), who uses bodily expression in the 'performance' of therapy, urges therapists to extend our 'Comfort Zone' and our repertoire of verbal and bodily language (p. 52).

I did not for a moment consider refusing Lottie's request for a hug; in any case it would have deprived both of us of something significant. When Lottie and I sat down again she said, 'That was more important than you realise.' And we smiled broadly at each other. The language of our physical contact was significant because of everything that had gone before: Lottie's life experiences had made my 'black cloud' comment particularly hurtful; her decision to 'confront' me, the way I had responded and the way the conversation had developed in such a surprising way combined to create something that was magical. The hug was mutually therapeutic; it was a way of expressing gratitude to each other that mere words could never have achieved.

Talking about clients and writing about them

Spoken and written language are interrelated because we are immersed in our social worlds (Jacques Derrida 1998: p. 29). What do we write about clients and what do we say about them in their absence when we are talking with other professionals? Peter Lang (2007) suggests that a useful question is, 'How would I like my doctor to talk about me when I am not there?' Therapists, he says, could consider the idea of drawing up a contract with every client as part of the work. We could seek consent from the client about *what* we will say and *how* we will talk about them, and what we will write about them. If we took this idea seriously, such a contract would have to be renewed often. Written documents are particularly potent because many follow clients for years, decades and even in some cases, generations.

Therapists are powerful agents in the process of co-creating stories about people. Reflecting on the language we use *about* clients when we write about them can have far-reaching effects. Involving clients in the language we use in our notes and reports gives clients the opportunity to become part of the process. If therapists and trainees do not share the report-writing process with clients, Janine Roberts (2005) says, mistakes and inaccuracies cannot be corrected; their story is 'co-opted'. Clients won't have ownership over records that others read and use to make decisions about them (p. 50).

At our first meeting we had jointly created some notes and I gave Lottie the typed version at our second meeting and invited her to alter anything if she wished. She said it was 'spot on' and she was delighted that I had described her as 'a bright woman' who was using her experiences of personal struggle to develop a vision of a better life in the future.

Conversations have an 'afterlife'

Every conversation has an afterlife, says Hilda Carpenter (2006, cited in Pearce 2007: p. 2).

The off-the-cuff remark I had made about the 'black cloud' had an 'afterlife' for Lottie; she wrestled for weeks with what I had meant by it. When she came to talk to me this enabled us to have a more helpful conversation which eclipsed the earlier one. At the end of this conversation I asked her to tell me if the process had been helpful and she said, 'talking about things that are bothering you can be healing'.

The conversations I'd had with Lottie have reverberated and touched me; they had a powerful 'afterlife', as this account shows. Lottie sent me a Thank You card recently, six months after we stopped meeting, showing that our conversations had an afterlife for her too. She thanked me in particular 'for the hugs'.

Reflexive questions

Reflecting on a conversation with a client in which there was a misunderstanding:

- Reflect on the conversational turns each of you took.
- What important metaphors and words did you use?
- Choose a key word and reflect on the different meanings it has for each of you.
- Did you and your client agree or differ about these meanings?
- How did your tone of voice, gestures and bodily language add to or contradict what you meant to 'say'?
- How did the client respond to these?
- What did your clothes, jewellery, skin colour and so on communicate to the client?

4
HOW STORIES OF TIME AFFECT OUR CONVERSATIONS

Ideas about time, such as how long a person 'needs' to complete a task, the 'right' time in one's life to achieve something and how long it should take for therapeutic change to take place are, like everything else, influenced by our culture, historical place in time, professional and personal presuppositions and so on.

We have seen how important it is for reflexive therapists to pay attention to our emotions and our language; now I explore how these stories about time affect our therapeutic conversations. Meanings co-evolve over time and therapists' and clients' stories interweave in mutually influential ways, and it is important to question our presuppositions about time as we do about everything else because therapists usually have more power in the relationship than do clients.

In this chapter I describe three approaches that helped my co-therapist and me develop self-reflexive practices in the conversations I discuss below.

(a) CMM (the Coordinated Management of Meaning);
(b) the concept of resonance;
(c) Kairon, from the Greek *kairos*, which relates to the idea of *timing*.

My colleague Heleni Andreadi and I had many conversations with Tomoko and her partner Graham in which we all re-appraised our different assumptions about time. Therapists' and clients' stories are mutually influential: some of Tomoko's stories about time resonated for me and some of Graham's stories about time resonated for Heleni, which helped us build unique bridges between us and them. These three concepts helped us work with Tomoko and Graham, who began to appreciate each other's different stories about time, enabling them to build a better relationship.

CMM, developed by Barnett Pearce and Vernon Cronen (W. B. Pearce and V. Cronen 1980; Cronen 2003; Pearce 2007), is an immensely useful 'practical theory' that helps us to explore how clients co-create their meanings with others, attempting to describe their patterns of communication, explain how they are co-constructed and how we can intervene to create 'better' patterns (Barnett Pearce 1999: p. 10). CMM also helps us explore and develop reflexivity about how our stories interweave with clients' stories.

Resonance helps therapists maintain reflexivity about the stories and themes we are connecting with as we talk with clients, and if a client's story resonates with one of ours we can use this to create a powerful bridge between us (Elkaim 1990). Our initial resonances may not be 'accurate' and a reflexive therapist is always prepared to be sensitive enough to let go of any resonance that could be ineffective or potentially harmful.

Kairos is: the 'right and proper time'; this relates to 'the propitious moment for the performance of an action or the coming into being of a new state' (*Oxford English Dictionary* 1989: pp. 340–1). The art of doing good therapy involves good timing: do we make an intervention or hold back, respond to something the client has just said, ask a question, offer an idea, refer to something that has resonated for us, make a joke or communicate in any other way?

Heleni and I noticed that ideas introduced early on were only taken up by Tomoko and Graham when the time was 'right' for them.

CMM: how meanings co-evolve over time

Barnett Pearce (1999) tells how, sitting round a campfire with friends in 1973, he coined the phrase the Coordinated Management of Meaning.

> Communication is about meaning . . . but not just in a passive sense of perceiving messages. Rather we live our lives filled with meanings, and one of our life challenges is to manage those meanings so that we can make our social worlds coherent and live within them with honor and respect. But this process of managing our meanings is never done in isolation. We are always . . . *coordinating* the way we manage our meanings with other people. So . . . communication is about the coordinated management of meaning.   (Pearce 1999)

He and Vernon Cronen (Pearce and Cronen 1980; V. Cronen 1994) collaborated for nearly twenty years to develop CMM: a 'practical theory' that foregrounds conjoint action and helps make sense of the way people's beliefs, stories, ideas and meanings are co-created within conversations. This has been immensely useful for therapists, enabling us to develop reflexive practices.

CMM helps therapists explore how clients' assumptions and stories create meaning in their life and affect the way they act; this focus on exploring clients' stories is described as a 'first order' position.

We can also use CMM to help us reflect on our own personal and professional presuppositions – how they interweave with clients' stories and the kinds of patterns we are co-creating with them. This 'second order' position is invaluable in helping us notice the way our presuppositions, language, emotions and so on influence the way the conversation evolves.

> Communication is the *primary* social reality . . . patterns of communication shape the persons that we are and the quality of our lives . . . the events and objects of our social worlds are 'made' in social processes of naming, calling, and interacting. (Pearce 1999: p. 10)

Exploring the *details* of conversations within a specific 'episode' helps therapists begin to understand the 'logic' of people's stories, and the meanings they give for their actions. In this way CMM helps us track, 'unpack' or deconstruct and eventually change unhelpful stories (Cronen 1990; 2000; Pearce and Cronen 1980; Cronen et al. 1989/1990).

Heleni had been working with Tomoko in individual therapy for some months; Tomoko often cried, saying she felt hopeless about herself and the future and she believed that certain things in her childhood 'explained' her distress. As well as being curious about these childhood and family experiences Heleni wanted to help Tomoko make sense of 'why now?' by exploring how her current relationships affected how she described the past and how they affected her view of the future.

Tomoko had been with her partner Graham for nine years and told Heleni that she was so exasperated with him that she was ready to leave. Heleni wondered whether something in the relationship was creating Tomoko's hopeless feelings about life, and made a tentative suggestion to invite Graham to come to the next meeting. Tomoko liked this idea and Graham readily agreed. Heleni then asked me to join them.

Meeting a client with a partner or family member helps us work with the communication processes, helping us track how certain stories have been co-created in these relationships. Working with another therapist can be tremendously energising, bringing forth a multitude of fresh stories that help therapists expand our presuppositions and question any strong and unhelpful patterns, so that we do not 'fall in love with' our hypothesis (Cecchin 1987: p. 412).

Heleni gave me some background information before I met them. Tomoko, in her late 30s, was several years older than Graham, who was in his mid-30s. They came from different cultures: Tomoko was Japanese, Graham was English. Tomoko had told Heleni that she wanted Graham to become 'more of a man' and although we didn't refer to this directly in the couple sessions it was useful information. Already Heleni and I were becoming curious about how their stories of age, gender, culture and ethnicity were affecting their relationship.

We agreed that Heleni would be the lead therapist, although we would work jointly and if I had an idea I could voice it at any time. This flexible, creative style worked well for us, although some therapists might prefer a more structured approach.

When I first saw them in the waiting area I noticed that Tomoko was a tiny, attractive Japanese woman with an open smile and Graham was a white man, similar in height and size to Tomoko, with a gentle manner. We all introduced ourselves, although of course Heleni and Tomoko already knew each other.

Heleni began by exploring their hopes for the conversation. Tomoko said she wanted Graham to change and take more responsibility; Graham said he wanted them to sort things out. I was curious about what his expectations of such a conversation might be, especially since Tomoko was so clear that she was not happy with him.

Heleni began by explore what they liked, appreciated and enjoyed about each other. They described sharing household chores, having long discussions about life, and going out to the cinema and concerts together. I was puzzled about what was making Tomoko so unhappy with Graham.

Heleni went on to ask about their hopes for the future. Instead of replying, Tomoko said she was tired, frustrated and fed up with things in the relationship; then she cried. Graham looked at her apprehensively. I got the idea that he was keener than Tomoko to stay in the relationship.

'What are the main frustrations?' Heleni asked. 'I don't trust him,' Tomoko said, adding that there had always been issues of trust between them.

The strength of CMM is that it enables therapists to explore how people co-create meaning together. Meaning is not seen as a private thing in the heads of private individuals but jointly produced in interaction. Speaking is not a reflection of what is in a person's mind; speaking and acting is an *embodied activity*. It is a performance and it is in that performance that we make our worlds; we create our realities. We put CMM into practice by exploring specific stories and episodes and using 'tools' such as 'circular' or relationship questioning, which help us explore how people's meanings co-evolve in sequences of interaction (Cecchin 1987; Carmel Fleuridas et al. 1986; Hedges 2005; Selvini Palazzoli et al. 1980).

I was wondering about 'trust': how did it show in the relationship? Did Tomoko mean that Graham was unfaithful, or not to be trusted with money, or something else entirely?

'Help us understand what Graham does that makes you not trust him?' Heleni asked.

'He doesn't keep his word,' Tomoko answered, 'he promises to do something but doesn't do it.'

'Are you surprised to hear Tomoko saying this?' Heleni asked Graham. He shook his head. He'd heard this before, he said, but he didn't agree with her. He insisted that he was trustworthy.

Heleni began to track how the issue of 'trust' and 'no trust' had evolved in the relationship over time.

'Give me an example of what he does or doesn't do that makes you not trust him,' she asked Tomoko. Tomoko said a good example was today, when they were coming for the appointment. They had originally planned to go to the shops in the afternoon, but had 'run out of time' and eventually had to hurry just to get here on time.

Heleni began to explore the details of the 'episode'.

Chronological time is an important aspect in CMM: by exploring an episode, specific moments in the client's life, therapist and client begin to make sense of the way these events unfold within sequences of actions. Episodes are bounded sequences of messages that have a narrative structure and are perceived as a unit (Pearce 1999). When we explore an 'episode' and ask about concrete events, we begin to notice how patterns of interaction evolve over time (p. 34).

To understand a communication we need to know what was said and/or done by whom and in what context BEFORE . . . what was said and/or done AFTER. . . . This way of looking at communication puts 'time' into the process and looks at things . . . as wholes.   (p. 26)

They were both at home during the day, Tomoko said; she had kept an eye on the time, so they would not be late for their appointment with us. At the same time she was trying to act differently, waiting, rather than getting angry with him. So she reminded him occasionally in a gentle way about the time. But this didn't work in getting him to pay attention to the time and they still missed getting to the shops.

'So, what was so engrossing that made you forget the time?' Heleni asked Graham, in a humorous way.

He smiled and said rather apologetically, 'I was on the computer'. He seemed to like Heleni's humorous tone, which otherwise could have made her question seem rather accusatory.

As I heard his answer I was making a connection to a personal story so I asked Graham whether he often became immersed in what he was doing.

'Yes,' he agreed; once he started doing something he would lose all sense of time.

'But you managed to get here on time,' Heleni said, laughing, 'how did that happen?'

Graham glanced at Tomoko and said, 'Tomoko got us here on time.'

'Wow!' Heleni said.

We all laughed. The atmosphere became lighter and Tomoko accepted the compliment.

'But,' Tomoko went on, 'it's maddening having to keep doing it.'

Even with her new approach, she said, it still amounted to the same thing: if she hadn't kept reminding Graham they wouldn't have got here on time. 'And nothing would ever get done,' she added.

Heleni and I broke off to have a brief 'reflecting team' conversation in front of the two of them.

Taking a respectful stance to explore dilemmas and paradoxical ideas, making connections to positively connote people's different positions, the 'reflecting team' (Tom Andersen 1987, 1990 and 1992) is an opportunity for clients to hear therapists' ideas. Clients can then respond and join the conversation.

As Tomoko and Graham listened, fascinated, we noted that this was a strong relationship that had lasted a long time and that Graham appreciated the way that Tomoko had taken responsibility for getting them to the appointment on time. Something must be working, we said. We shared our prejudice that we both wanted to help them stay together and make the relationship work. Maybe Tomoko was 'highly organised' and Graham was more 'laid-back'. Was this was to do with male and female styles, or did it relate to their different cultural stories? Maybe Graham was 'over-optimistic' about time, I said. Perhaps he enjoys this position, Heleni said. Yet it wasn't working for Tomoko, I responded, and it was having a detrimental effect on the future of the relationship.

'What did you like hearing?' Heleni asked them. 'What made sense for you?'

Graham agreed that he was over-optimistic about time and that when he became immersed in doing something he would forget about everything else.

'It's deeper than that,' Tomoko interrupted. She mentioned the issue of trust again, adding that Graham was 'wasting time'. 'This has been going on for nine years – since we met,' she said.

Stories of work, success and time

Heleni began to explore how they had met and what had attracted them to each other. They'd met in London, Tomoko said. She'd been living here for some time, and had just left an unsatisfactory relationship and a business she'd run with her ex-partner, thus losing her home and her source of income in one stroke. When she met Graham she was not looking for a relationship but had been attracted to him.

Graham had come to London from the provinces. He'd enjoyed being a 'free agent', leading an easy-going life of pubs and clubs. He was also not looking for a relationship but when he met Tomoko he'd fallen for her. And they'd been together ever since.

As well as their coming from totally different countries and cultures, their families were different: Tomoko's parents were successful, entrepreneurial and creative. She had come from Japan alone, had found a job and a place to live right away; she was adventurous. Graham's parents were semi-

skilled workers; he was still closely involved with them and hadn't strayed far from home.

Tomoko returned to her dissatisfaction with Graham, saying she was fed up with always being the one who organised things, always 'having to nag' and 'push him' to get anything done.

'What if you don't "push", "organise" and "nag"'? Heleni asked. 'Things just wouldn't get done,' Tomoko said.

'We are always in more than one conversation,' says Barnett Pearce (1999). 'Everything we say has multiple meanings in the various conversations of which we are a part . . . we are enmeshed in multiple conversations simultaneously' (p. 33). Exploring an episode using CMM helps us 'unpack', or deconstruct these multiple stories.

The 'hierarchical' CMM model (Figures 1 and 2) shows the complexity of what is happening at any one moment; one story can become the 'highest context' affecting other stories. Therapists explore in detail the different 'voices' and stories influencing how each person acts.

CMM helps therapists identify the numerous complex stories that can become intertwined within an episode:

(1) There are an indeterminate number of levels of context: culture, society, religion, gender, family, self-identity, relationship and so on.
(2) The position of various levels of context is not fixed. And they can shift.

Tomoko and Graham's stories were particularly rich because of the contrast between their different cultural, gender and family stories.

For us to unravel and make sense of all the different aspects of each of their stories took time. The family story of achievement and 'success' seemed to be the 'highest context' for Tomoko; it organised her stories about her relationship with Graham and whether he was enough of 'a man' for the relationship to work long-term. It was different for Graham: his relationship with Tomoko was the higher context: his relationship influenced his stories of money and success in his work.

Tomoko and Graham's relationship stories had evolved over time: when they had first met neither was looking for a relationship but they were 'smitten' by each other. In this they had seemed similar, but difficulties had arisen because of their totally different, and incompatible, stories of success, exemplified by their stories of time.

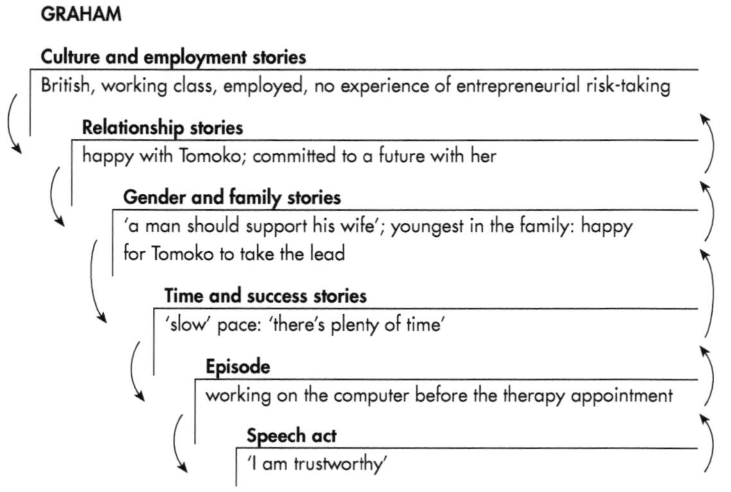

GRAHAM

Culture and employment stories

British, working class, employed, no experience of entrepreneurial risk-taking

Relationship stories

happy with Tomoko; committed to a future with her

Gender and family stories

'a man should support his wife'; youngest in the family: happy for Tomoko to take the lead

Time and success stories

'slow' pace: 'there's plenty of time'

Episode

working on the computer before the therapy appointment

Speech act

'I am trustworthy'

Figure 1   CMM: hierarchical model of Graham's initial stories

CMM helps us explore the taken-for-granted stories that form the backdrop and permeate people's lives; what they consider 'normal', the 'rules', 'shoulds' and 'oughts' about how to behave. Family and community stories are powerful ways in which we learn to become members of our culture: even if we rebel against them, we are immersed in these values and norms.

There were tensions in their different stories about gender: Tomoko had told Heleni about a time when a drunken man harassed a woman and Graham hadn't intervened. This, she said, showed that he was not 'a real man'. But Graham's gender identity story didn't include putting himself in danger.

Tomoko thought 'a real man' should be successful in his work – yet another area of frustration with Graham. 'He's always moaning about his job,' she said, 'but he doesn't do anything about it. I'm fed up.' He'd been talking for months about going freelance, promising to follow up contacts, but had found reasons not to. The trip to the shops that day was to buy office supplies for his freelance business. This gave us an important clue: she was frustrated and angry when Graham was not making progress in his freelance career.

I wondered whether Graham had a story that there was 'plenty of time' to make a success in his career. Did Tomoko have a story that there wasn't

much time because she was older than him? Did this explain her push to get him to 'get on with things'? Graham agreed that he complained about work; he did want to go freelance, he said hesitantly, but in the small-knit community of his field of work he'd made mistakes, his reputation was not good and his colleagues didn't value him. Going freelance would test his standing in the field. Tomoko didn't agree and reminded him of positive things colleagues had been saying about his work.

Tomoko was doing a degree in order to create a future and eventually earn a good salary. She didn't want to be financially dependent on Graham, so why, she asked, didn't he get on and make his freelance career a reality?

Tomoko and Graham's different gender, family and cultural stories were influential in determining how they responded to each other and how they saw time. 'Success' was the 'highest context' for Tomoko; 'relationship with Tomoko', the highest context for Graham. Family stories supported Tomoko's initial approach to success, time and risk-taking: her father was creative and entrepreneurial; her mother, the 'woman behind the successful man'. A strong story in the family was, 'success comes when you make things happen'. This get-up-and-go attitude was not typical in Japanese culture.

Graham's father was the breadwinner in their family; his family story was 'a man should support his wife'. There was no experience of risk-taking or being entrepreneurial in his family and this made him unwilling to give up a 'safe' job and risk going freelance.

We wondered if stories of age may have influenced how each of them responded to time. Graham was in his early 30s; maybe he thought 'there's plenty of time'? Tomoko was in her late 30s. Did she have a story that time was running out? At her age her father was a successful artist. An important and influential story was that she was frustrated with herself because she was not getting on with her own studies. Her family stories of success and risk-taking and her identity stories influenced her disappointment and frustration with herself for not being successful.

Tomoko was impatient with the time Graham took to do day-to-day tasks and, more broadly, the time he seemed to need to make a life change.

Other models of CMM

The 'atomic' or 'daisy' model (Figure 3) is another way of using CMM; more like a 'snapshot' in time, this helps therapists to plot important stories within a particular episode. It shows the numerous conversations within one episode but doesn't show how new stories develop over time (Barnett Pearce 1999: p. 55; Hedges 2005: pp. 51–2).

We could plot the different stories involved in the episode Tomoko and Graham first talked about: the afternoon when they had come for the appointment, her stories of time and family stories of just 'get on and do it' which made her do a degree and encourage Graham to leave his job, where he was unhappy. Graham wanted to please Tomoko; he wanted to leave his hated job and go freelance but wanted to 'play it safe' and earn money to support them both, and this made him afraid to take the plunge.

Systemic therapist Peter Lang (2008), who worked closely on developing CMM with Vernon Cronen and Barnett Pearce, prefers the metaphor of stories being woven together in a context; the Latin word *con-text* means 'to weave'. This more fluid description shows how therapists' and clients' stories interweave and influence each other; some stories become stronger in certain contexts whilst others disappear and fade, like threads in a woven piece of cloth. We can visualise how a delicate blue thread in a fabric is enhanced if it is flanked by other subtle colours or contrasted with a dark colour. But a pale blue thread disappears when put next to a scarlet or fluorescent orange thread. In this way subtle stories can become eclipsed in a particular context. Or 'loud' stories can dominate 'quieter' stories.

Therapists' stories about time

Time and space are primary distinctions that therapists make (Luigi Boscolo and Paulo Bertrando 1996). Therapists differ in their expectations about how long it should take for change to take place and this will affect how often we meet with a client and how long we think the work will take before the client no longer 'needs' therapy. Each therapeutic approach has a different and 'often a non-articulated position with regard to the role of time in the formation and resolution of human dilemmas' (Paul Gibney 1994: p. 61, in Boscolo and Bertrando 1996: p. 58). 'Therapists used to long-term therapy tend to create the conditions for a protracted therapy', they say (p. 59). It is useful to understand whether the client's temporal horizon faces backwards into the past (e.g. in depression), is locked exclusively into the present time, or is open to both past and future' (p. 61).

It is a myth that therapeutic change needs to take a lot of time; new meanings or a new connection can emerge fully-formed in a flash. A long period of time is not always needed for a new idea to occur (Lang 2008).

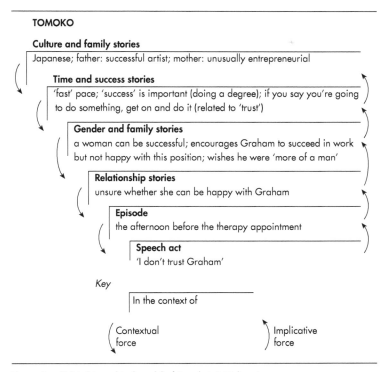

Figure 2   CMM: hierarchical model of Tomoko's initial stories

Heleni and I did not expect to meet with this couple every week. Our experience with other clients and what we noticed about Tomoko and Graham's willingness to discuss their difficulties and listen to each other made us feel hopeful that they would be able to resolve their difficulties with just a little help from us. We described ourselves as catalysts rather than instigators of change and didn't encourage them to depend on us.

As Tomoko explored her relationship with Graham with us she shifted her focus from the past to the present; Graham's focus was on the present and as we explored their many stories he began to make plans for the future. And as both of them began to understand each other's stories about time they both began to feel more hopeful about the future of their relationship and the possibility of success in their lives.

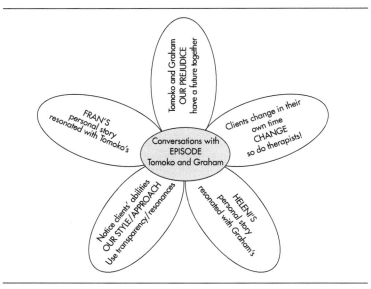

Figure 3 CMM: 'atomic' or 'daisy' model: Heleni and Fran's stories of time

Stories that resonate

The concept of resonance is invaluable for reflexive therapists. Taking notice of what resonates for us is crucial for the development of therapy, according to Mony Elkaim (1990). When we make an emotional connection with a client's story it is as if some kind of reverberation is taking place; our feelings appear to echo the client's. Resonance occurs 'when the same rule or feeling appears to be present in different but related systems' (p. xxi). It is created by the intersection of different systems that include a common element; it is as if when we notice similar stories within the clients' stories and our own, a kind of vibration takes place.

Aspects of Tomoko and Graham's stories resonated for Heleni and me. When Tomoko spoke of her frustration with having to remind Graham about the time, this resonated for me. I connected with a personal experience of being with an ex-partner who often 'forgot the time', turned up late and took a long time to do things. I, like Tomoko, had tried different ways to change him.

When I noticed this I asked Heleni if I could say something. She nodded eagerly. Taking a risk I told Tomoko and Graham of my experience in that relationship and how hurt, upset and frustrated by this behaviour I was and how I'd felt un-loved and un-valued.

Before I had finished, Tomoko interrupted in an excited way to thank me. 'I can tell that you really understand me,' she said. 'I don't feel so strange and bad about myself.' Graham listened, fascinated. He said, 'I see . . .', in a thoughtful way as if he was hearing something new.

Resonances arise in 'couplings': what the therapist and client co-construct between us. Something moves us and this is 'at the intersection' of what seems important to the therapist as well as the client. We make a connection with something important in the clients' story and this intersection creates a bridge between us. What each person, including the therapist, experiences in a therapeutic system is 'both linked to themselves and not reducible to them' (Elkaim 1990: p. 130). When a story resonates with us the feelings that arise are unique, but what is felt is amplified and maintained by the context in which we find ourselves, being simply the visible part of a much larger system that can include professional, organisational and cultural stories as well as personal ones.

Showing Tomoko and Graham the way their story resonated for me had a profound effect on both of them. Tomoko, who had previously felt guilty about being frustrated with Graham, said she began to feel more 'normal', whilst Graham seemed to understand Tomoko's frequent angry outbursts differently. However, Graham's position resonated more for Heleni. She said she wished she could be laid-back like him, able to allow things to unfold in their own time; she admired his ability to become so engrossed in a task that he could forget the time.

She offered this resonance to them, noting that there was 'merit in trusting that things would unfold in their own time', and that 'being able to concentrate so well to the exclusion of everything else is quite a skill, whilst being organised and focused are also invaluable skills to help one succeed in our society'.

Another important story resonated for Heleni: her partner had recently made a decision that involved a change in their relationship, which he expected her to follow. Graham's position resonated for her because he was the one being asked to change. She said to me, as Tomoko and Graham listened intently, 'What if Tomoko slowed down, and allowed Graham to catch up with her?'

This helped Tomoko take a different position towards Graham's actions, and non-actions. And it helped Graham feel acknowledged and appreciated.

As the conversation progressed I became aware that the three of us were focused on Graham, exploring his dilemmas, encouraging, offering suggestions and so on. What pattern were we re-creating? I recalled that he was the youngest in his family with two older sisters and a mother. I broke in to say to him, 'I've noticed something fascinating: here we are, three older women offering you all kinds of suggestions, trying to help you. Does this feel familiar?'

'Yes!' Graham said in an unusually decisive way. And we all burst out laughing. He told us that both his sisters and his mother often tried to help him sort things out.

'Do you like this?' I asked.

'Yes!' he replied in such a firm way that we all laughed again.

The danger in offering this observation was that Graham could have felt offended by the idea that there was an alliance between the three of us, all women. But by identifying what was resonating for me I demonstrated that I was willing to accept my part in the co-construction of this 'reality'.

'Do you offer him help and advice too? Heleni asked Tomoko.

'Yes,' she said, thoughtfully.

Being transparent about our resonances and the pattern we had inadvertently re-created in the conversation turned out to be crucial in helping Tomoko and Graham notice an aspect of their own pattern of interaction. It became a major turning point. Graham recognised his tendency to invite others to help him resolve his dilemmas. He acknowledged his part in co-creating this pattern in his relationship with Tomoko. And Tomoko realised that she had responded to his 'invitation'.

The value of resonance is that when we work on one point of resonance, change seems to take place in other parts of the system. Resonances can involve the therapist's family of origin, supervision and broader sociocultural and political elements including the institutional system, Elkaim claims. 'It is far richer, to think about the function and meaning of the feeling experienced in relation to the whole system' (p. 9).

This demonstration of reflexivity and a 'second order' position was, fortunately, well timed. It came towards the end of our first conversation, after we had shown that we could appreciate both their positions. The conversation ended in a more hopeful way than it had begun.

Allowing changes to evolve over time

Therapists often need patience and optimism about the time needed for clients to change their stories at their own pace and in their own time-frame.

At the second meeting, a month later, Tomoko and Graham told us that their landlady was selling the house and they would have to leave their flat, which was a shock. Tomoko thought this was an opportunity to go their separate ways. This was because, although Graham had handed in his notice at work, he was planning to take freelance work from the company he'd been working for rather than severing all ties with them. She was disappointed in him and thought this was rather cowardly. As well as acknowledging Tomoko's frustration, Heleni and I applauded Graham's courageousness and noted that he was starting his business and making sure that he earned enough to support them both.

At the third meeting, a month after that, Graham said he'd been reflecting on his way of inviting people to help him offer solutions to his dilemmas. He was beginning to do things for himself rather than expecting others to help him. Also, he said, originally he'd only come with Tomoko to help her. He implied that her dissatisfaction with him was her problem. But now he realised that he was learning things that were useful for both of them and he'd actually looked forward to coming this time.

Tomoko said she was pleased with how everything was going.

At the fourth meeting, another month later, Graham took the lead, which was unusual. He said that they'd just moved into a new flat together. Both of them looked and sounded excited and happy.

And Graham had made a surprising new connection. 'Now I understand what Tomoko meant by trust,' he said. He went on to tell us that he'd promised to get the deposit money from the bank to pay the new landlady and he'd done it with just fifteen minutes to spare. Previously he might not have 'got it together'. Tomoko had allowed him to do this without constant reminders. And he now understood that Tomoko wanted him to keep his word; she wanted to rely on him to do what he'd agreed to do and this is what she meant by 'trust'.

It had taken him some time to make this connection, one that we had actually made in the first meeting. We'd had to allow him to realise this in his own time. It was an exciting moment for the four of us.

One of the tasks of therapy is to say something that will help clients recall what they already know, so that they see the familiar in a new way.

'Is it something about "follow through"?' I asked Graham. 'Follow through' was another idea we had explored in the first meeting.

'Absolutely,' Tomoko said. And Graham smiled at her.

Heleni and I were thrilled and turned to each other, saying, 'He's got it! He's seen the light!' We all laughed and Graham and Tomoko beamed and gazed at each other in a loving way.

Going on to describe the move to the new flat in more detail, they told us that they had each taken responsibility for different tasks, working separately yet in tandem. Whilst Tomoko was cleaning the new flat, Graham and their friends had shifted the boxes. They hadn't seen much of each other during the day and had met afterwards to celebrate their success.

This was an exciting new story. Tomoko had trusted Graham to get on and do what he'd promised to do: he was 'a real man'. She didn't need to keep reminding him to get on with things, so could relax. Heleni and I observed that each of them had done something different, working together, trusting each other to get the task done. Was Graham becoming 'a real man' in Tomoko's eyes?

New stories of time

'We each have a different pace,' Tomoko said, 'I can't expect him to work in the same way as me.'

'This time,' she added, 'I held back, allowed him to do the things at his own pace. And Graham had repaid her by keeping his promises.

Graham said that he had finally left his job, explaining more firmly than before that working freelance for the same company made sense; as he was developing his contacts he could build his business reputation gradually.

It was something Heleni and I couldn't have predicted. We were impressed with both of them. Tomoko had begun to accept that Graham was doing things in his own way and in his own time-frame and he'd 'followed through' with the practical tasks necessary for setting up the business.

'It seemed as if, at first, you were both at opposite ends of a spectrum,' I said, holding my two fists a long way apart, showing the distance between them. 'Your ideas about time and how long it should take to do things were miles apart. Now,' I moved my fists closer together, 'you're coming together.' They both nodded vigorously, smiling.

Now Tomoko told us that she'd done something new and amazing: she'd been able to make a phone call to inquire about a new job. I didn't know that she'd any difficulty with making phone calls, although this was something Heleni and Graham knew.

'Graham had to make the calls to chase up bills,' Tomoko told me. 'But he always took too long.' This had been intensely frustrating. This new information changed my stories about them dramatically. Maybe Tomoko's irritation with Graham's slowness had been as much to do with frustration with herself and her own difficulty with making phone calls?

Then Heleni and I began to explore their different ideas about competence in another brief 'reflecting team' conversation. Both of them were able to identify each other's abilities, we said; they had different, complementary, abilities and were able to help each other.

'I used to have the idea that Tomoko was the competent one,' I said, and hesitated, looking across at Graham.

'Go on,' he said, 'you can say anything you like.'

'And Graham was seen as the "incompetent" one,' I said to Heleni. 'Now it seems like there's sometimes a reversal.' I made a cross-over gesture with my hands. 'You can be competent in different ways and at different times.'

We went on to notice the way they had come to value each other's approaches to time; Tomoko valued Graham's ability to take time to make changes and Graham valued Tomoko's get-up-and-go approach to making changes.

'I've noticed,' Heleni said, 'Graham's much more playful today. He's talking more, added things, joining in the conversation with us more.'

'Yes,' Graham said, he did feel more part of things and it was becoming easier to talk. Tomoko looked fondly at him.

I had also shifted my stories about Tomoko and Graham. What I had described as Graham's frustratingly 'relaxed' attitude had resonated with a personal story. Now I admired the way that the 'higher context' of loyalty to supporting Tomoko influenced his stories of work and success.

What we had described as Tomoko's rather 'pushy' approach we could now describe as an ability to focus and help both of them to accomplish things. Tomoko told us that her part-time job meant that she could now contribute financially to the household, which made her feel better about herself. Also she'd begun to focus on her academic work, which she'd neglected. And Graham had accepted that Tomoko's earnings would help him develop his freelance business: they were working on a shared future.

Tomoko wanted to continue to explore her family and personal stories in individual therapy; she told Heleni that she was less frustrated with Graham, that he was developing his business in his own time-frame and she was happy with this; she described him as providing the stability that she needed. It was interesting that having been initially reluctant to come to therapy he reported how grateful he was for the way it had helped them save their relationship.

Reflexive questions

Thinking about a client with whom you are working:

- Are your and your client's ideas about time similar or different?
- What is your, and their, primary focus: present, future or past?
- How long do you expect to work with them?
- When do you expect to notice any significant and positive changes in the way the client feels and lives their life?
- How do you and the client decide about how often you meet – do you negotiate this?
- If any of the client's stories resonated for you, how did you use this resonance?
- What was your client's response?

5

TRANSPARENCY AND SELF-DISCLOSURE

Therapists are always disclosing aspects of themselves to clients; much is unavoidable, some is accidental and some may be deliberate.

In this chapter I describe how I wrestled with whether to risk telling my client Leanne that, like her, I'd had a complex relationship with my mother. This self-disclosure proved to be a turning point in the therapy.

Clients reported that self-disclosure was the most helpful out of 32 different types of therapist intervention (Janine Roberts 2005: p. 58). However, it must be used tentatively and with care, must be value and theory driven and must always be in the client's best interests, she says.

Positioning 'theory' (Rom Harré and Luk van Langenhove 1999) is invaluable in helping reflexive therapists reflect on inherent power differentials between us and the client, how we could be positioning them by what we say or don't say, which can affect the client's important relationships.

A 'dialogical' way of working is one that makes our knowledge available to clients as we share and learn from each other, Peter Lang (2009) says. Telling stories about how other clients and families responded to struggles (keeping confidentiality, of course) introduces clients to a broader range of ideas and stories, which co-creates hope. Similarly, he says, supervisors enliven the supervision process by illustrating theory with stories from practice.

There are dangers and many benefits when we deliberately reveal something personal to a client: this can make a powerful connection with a client and can lessen the separation between us. But it involves taking a risk and requires highly sophisticated abilities of self-reflexivity. A deliberate self-disclosure can shift clients from a one-down position to a more egalitarian one that acknowledges that we are all challenged in various ways throughout our life.

When I first met twenty-three-year-old Leanne there was much that she could glean from my appearance, speech and so on; the pictures and objects in the room and the state of my desk also revealed things about me. I encouraged her to ask me questions, used deliberate self-disclosure where appropriate and shared my therapeutic ideas with her.

We cannot avoid revealing some aspects of ourselves, such as our gender, colour, bodily shape and size, pregnancy, and differing abilities (deafness, blindness, a limp and so on). And our clothes, jewellery and hairstyle, how we speak, our accent, cadence and tone of voice can reveal a lot about us. The place where we work can reveal our status and position; if we practise from home this can reveal a great deal about class and economic status. When therapists work in an organisation or residential setting, or live in a small community, there is more chance of unplanned encounters outside the therapy room and these accidental self-disclosures can be problematic or beneficial.

I worked in a University Counselling Service and when Leanne and I accidentally bumped into each other one day, I waited for her to acknowledge me, in case she didn't want anyone to know that she was coming to see me. When she smiled and said 'hello' I responded warmly.

Brief historical overview

Sigmund Freud (1953) advocated that the 'physician should be impenetrable to the patient, and like a mirror, reflect nothing but what is shown to him'. However, as analytic psychotherapist Patrick Casement (1985) says, 'Analysts and therapists often give away more about themselves than they realize . . . patients scrutinize the analyst, who aims to remain inscrutable, and they find many clues to the nature of this person they are dealing with' (p. 58).

In the 1960s humanistic therapists challenged therapists' aim of not revealing themselves, and argued that deliberate self-disclosure could be therapeutic and valuable (Sidney Jourard 1971). In the 1970s and 1980s the feminist movement advocated more egalitarian relationships between therapist and client (Laura Brown 1994). Transparency and self-disclosure, from a feminist perspective, affirms women's shared experiences, demystifies therapy, decreases hierarchy, and acknowledges power differentials.

These and other political ideas influenced family therapy and eventually family teams began to talk in front of clients rather than talking about them behind the one-way mirror. Tom Andersen (1990) developed his 'reflecting team' model where therapists invited families to switch places, to respond and comment on the team's discussions. Michael White (1995), using Narrative approaches, actively encouraged therapists to be transparent about their ideas and political positions.

In the 1990s social and cultural shifts encouraged people to talk publicly about themselves on television shows. Since then the cult of celebrity and the reality television genre has taken personal disclosure to another level. Clients and patients are now being described as 'consumers', encouraged to make choices and question the expertise of service providers, although this is still work in progress. Recent technological developments such as the internet have made information about therapists more readily available.

'Invitational inquiry'

Janine Roberts's (2005) 'invitational inquiry' approach encourages therapists to be transparent with clients. From the outset she will talk about 'working as a good team', welcoming discussion about all aspects of the therapy: the format of sessions and their 'stances about change and healing' (p. 55).

Family therapist Harlene Anderson (1997) also encourages therapists to be open about relevant aspects of their personal and professional stories and invites clients to ask her questions. Instead of using the term 'transparent', when therapists choose to disclose aspects of ourselves, she says we are making something public rather than being private or secret. This is:

> more readily revealing, more readily sharing out loud my private inner dialogues and monologues: my thoughts, prejudices, wonderings, speculations, questions, opinions, and fears. And, in doing so, opening myself to feedback, evaluation and critique. Consequently I expose myself more as a person to all those with whom I work.   (pp. 102–3)

Deciding whether to reveal a view or explore the way our clients are affecting us takes skill and sensitivity. Therapists may find this a challenge: they may have personal, family or cultural stories about being open or not, or they may believe they don't have the ability to take such a 'risk'. However, rather than waiting for trust to develop before taking such a 'risk' we can create intimacy and even more trust, according to Barry Mason (2005), who writes extensively about therapists' risk-taking. All therapists have personal, family and cultural experiences that can become invaluable resources in our work, which we can use to help us build bridges between us and the client. After practising for some years, therapists will have heard many hundreds of stories and will have a vast library of knowledge about the creative ways that people respond to difficulties. This provides a rich storehouse of information which can expand the number of stories to which clients have access. It is important not to marginalise aspects of our own expertise, Barry Mason says, as this could potentially do 'a disservice to our clients'. When we own our own position and our expertise or explore something risky, it is useful to do this from a position of 'authoritative doubt' rather than 'authoritative certainty' (p. 162). Similarly, supervisors who do not offer their own ideas do a disservice to supervisees.

Being open with a client can help shift an impasse, Peter Rober (1999) suggests. For example, during a difficult conversation with a family, he had been angry with the father, who he experienced as 'rigid'. Afterwards he felt 'bad' and 'worthless as a therapist'. After a discussion with a colleague he made a heartfelt apology and was able to be open about his feelings with the father at the next family meeting. This led to a freer conversation and the father made an important revelation which helped others in the family understand his behaviour.

Transparency about our moral and political positions

Some months after we had begun working together, just as things were improving for Leanne, she came into our session looking pale and drawn. After a silence she told me haltingly that something dreadful had happened. Stumbling over her words, she said that she had been raped. I felt shock and anger that a stranger had hurt her.

Rather than wondering whether to make a self-disclosure, supervisors and teachers who train therapists need to discuss whether not disclosing something might damage the therapeutic process, Elsa Jones (1993) believes. Therapist and client are always in unequal power positions; therapists are on home territory whilst clients are not. 'The client is by definition unhappy, confused or uncertain, and is coming to discuss private matters with a stranger. . . . It is a one-sided intimacy . . . the client is expected to be self-revealing and the therapist is not, or certainly not to the same degree or about the same topics' (p. 155). She warns against moral neutrality, particularly when we encounter power differentials such as in sex abuse. The question of how to respond is more relevant than whether to speak up (pp. 146–7).

I viewed my reactions as resources. First I thanked her for telling me about what had happened, noting that this was the first time she had confided in someone so soon. Leanne had been sexually abused by her father and had kept this a secret all her childhood and adolescence. By telling me about the rape, she was doing something new.

With her permission I explored what had happened. The man, she said, had singled her out at a friend's house party and persuaded her to go outside. Then he had dragged her into thick shrubs and, ignoring her pleas and struggles, had raped her.

Leanne twisted her scarf in her hands as she told me that since the rape she'd been taking scalding showers, scrubbing her body punitively and had self-harmed by cutting herself. She'd been asking herself over and over whether she had struggled hard enough and why the man had singled her out. She berated herself for not shouting out or screaming. Maybe she'd been 'to blame'? I felt sorry for what had happened, the way she was hurting herself and her endless self-questioning.

Narrative therapist Michael White (2007) encourages therapists to be clear with clients about the origins of our ideas. People's personal narratives are shaped by socially constructed norms mandated by power relations inherent within certain institutions: 'ideas about dysfunction and psychopathology obscure the complexities associated with human action, many of which arise from the actual contexts of people's lives' (p. 267). Therapists are influential in our society and we can use our influence to challenge the 'discourses of domination' that we are steeped in, and which 'subjugate' certain people. However, family therapist Jim Wilson (2007) says that 'the ideal of the entirely transparent therapeutic relationship is misplaced and disingenuous' (p. 36).

I wanted to challenge Leanne's belief that she was 'bad' and to blame for what had happened. After listening to her agonised self-questioning I decided to be transparent about my outrage. 'No man has the right to force himself on a woman,' I said. 'That man had no right to violate you.' I was transparent and chose these words for their shock value. I talked about the inequality in their physical size and strength and the myth that a woman who says 'No' really means 'Yes'. Leanne listened keenly and nodded.

By saying that the rape was not OK I was being transparent about my own values and making my moral position clear: no person has the right to force another to have sex against their will, I said. Having done this I checked out what effect my words had had on her.

'What d'you think about what I've just said?' I asked. She fixed me with a direct look and said, 'It's a relief.' She went on to explain that because I'd been so clear, this would stop her becoming ensnared in knots of self-blame. I noticed that she had relaxed and was not twisting the scarf any more.

Leanne had been struggling with the idea that she may have been to 'blame' for the rape because she hadn't screamed or called out for help at the time. I reminded her that her father had effectively taught her not to make any sound during the abuse which took place in the family home; he had the power to keep her silent throughout her childhood and adolescence.

The familiar position of self-doubt and self-hatred had some logic because her father had encouraged her to view herself as complicit in the sex-abuse he'd perpetrated. But she could change that now.

Not to attend to social inequities and myths such as men's 'ungovernable sex drive', which are as influential as family events and personal stories, can mean that we are '(silently) condoning them' (Elsa Jones 1993). Many people find that 'expressions of personal agency are . . . limited because they are subject to traditional power relations that are institutionalized in local culture . . . power relationship of disadvantage, of race, of gender, heterosexism, of culture, of ethnicity, and more' (White 2007: p. 267). In systemic therapy the context of political and sociocultural forces that shape people's realities is always in focus, Jim Wilson (2007) says, although the therapist's motivation is not to raise political awareness (p. 62).

Leanne's father had been successful in spoiling her relationship with her mother throughout those years by keeping the abuse secret and creating a relationship with Leanne that encouraged rivalry between her and her mother. But eventually Leanne had spoken out. Disclosing the abuse when she was seventeen signified tremendous courage and thankfully her mother believed her. I described this as a way that she had become empowered (Imelda McCarthy and Nollaig Byrne 1988).

I explored the subtle ways that Leanne had rebelled against the abuse: she described turning her head away and using her imagination to metaphorically remove herself from what was happening to her body; sometimes called 'disassociation'. She had also created an imaginary 'finger family' in which each finger was based on someone in her family. Being transparent about my moral position helped Leanne to question her belief that she was complicit in the abuse.

I was inspired by the idea of identifying 'moments of liberation' adapted by Peter Lang (2007) from Allen Wade's (1997) idea of 'moments of resistance', which describes the way people with little power find subtle ways to escape subjugation.

She loved describing herself as 'resisting' and the idea that her actions had been 'liberating'. I was open about where these ideas had come from and gave her a photocopy of Allen Wade's paper when she asked for it.

Positioning 'theory'

Positioning 'theory' is invaluable in helping therapists think about how the client and the therapist could be positioned if we decide to use deliberate self-disclosure. Introduced into the social sciences by Wendy Holloway (1984) in the construction of subjectivity in heterosexual relations, these ideas have been developed by Rom Harré (2008). Positioning 'theory', he says, shares many similarities with the communication model known as CMM: Coordinated Management of Meaning, discussed in Chapter 4.

Positioning is unlike the idea of taking a role, which is static; positions are ever-shifting within conversations; one of the most important contributions of positioning theory to psychology is the idea that our social worlds are fluid and are based on a set of shared meanings, dynamic and constantly and rapidly being renegotiated (Harré and van Langenhove 1999). 'Positioning always takes place within a specific moral order maintained within a specific context, such as a social group. It is through our social relations that social norms are regulated and passed on (Moghaddam 1999: p. 80). We can look at positions as a loose set of rights and duties that give meaning to one's actions.

Just as we cannot not communicate, we cannot not take a position: what a therapist says, or doesn't say, to a client always involves taking a position, which simultaneously positions the other person. Therapists and clients have different rights and duties and we can clarify them when we talk with clients.

Positions are always relational and positioning is frequently outside the power of those so positioned. For example, the speech acts of a person positioned as simple minded are not taken seriously in contemporary Western society (Rom Harré and Fathali Moghaddam 2003: p. 205). If someone positions themselves as a 'nurse', by taking care of someone, the other person will become positioned as a 'patient', 'whether they want it or not ... acting like a patient drives someone else into the nurse position' (pp. 5 –7). If a therapist positions themselves as the 'hero' who rides into a client's life on a metaphorical white charger, believing they will resolve all the client's difficulties, this positions the client as a grateful recipient.

Leanne and I occupied different positions with different rights, duties and responsibilities. Following my professional Code of Ethics my duty was to work in a helpful way with her. She was positioned by her father as compliant in the sex abuse, a person with minimal rights; he trained her not to make a sound during these acts and used many clever ways to drive a wedge between her and her mother to ensure that she would not divulge what was happening.

I wondered how I could be positioning Leanne in relation to her mother and wanted to explore this with her.

Position, speech acts and storyline

There are three interrelated aspects involved in 'positioning':

(a) a person's storyline;
(b) how we perform these storylines; and
(c) the rights and duties involved.   (Rom Harré 2008)

Every position involves a 'storyline': the story that we tell about what we are doing and what is happening (how we are performing these storylines).

A 'position' is a cluster of rights and duties within a context: each person has some rights to do certain things and is also prohibited from doing certain things in that context. In our daily life these rights, duties and obligations are converted into expectations and beliefs, 'oughts' and 'shoulds', which show how social positioning operates in our relationships.

Leanne's father positioned himself as:

- *powerful*
- *the 'good' one*
- *always in the 'right'*
- *Leanne's lover*

Leanne was positioned by her father as:

- *powerless*
- *the 'bad' one*

- *her father's lover*
- *her mother's rival*
- *complicit in the abuse*

To make her compliant he taught her that what was happening was normal in other families and that other children enjoyed it. As a child Leanne had few rights. Because she wanted the abuse to stop but didn't make a protest she developed a storyline that she must be 'bad' because she had 'chosen' to allow it to continue. During the rape and afterwards she revisited this position and the familiar storyline: 'I could have stopped it; I should have shouted out or screamed.' Leanne's storyline connects with certain myths in our culture which include stories such as, 'every woman has a fantasy that she wants to be raped' and 'she must have wanted it'.

Positioning theory offers therapists at least two invaluable tools; it helps us:

(a) explore clients' speech acts, de-construct their storylines and make sense of their positions;
(b) reflect on what we are saying (our speech), our storylines and the position we are taking vis-à-vis the client.

Position (a) relates to what is called a 'first-order' position, where a therapist focuses primarily on clients' stories and meaning and the actions in their relationships. This process helps a therapist explore the rights, duties and responsibilities involved in the client's relationships and how each person is positioned in relation to the other(s).

Position (b) relates to a 'second-order' position. When we meet a client we become part of their 'system': the therapist's and client's worlds entwine and our presuppositions and prejudices become mutually influential. A reflexive therapist considers how our 'storylines' (presuppositions) and 'speech acts' could be positioning the client. Therapists who are transparent with clients about their beliefs and values and are reflexive about their involvement in the co-creation of certain stories are taking a 'second-order position'.

I began to understand Leanne's meanings and storylines and the positions she had occupied in her family, which helped me appreciate the 'logic' of her responses to the rape. I was transparent about the position I took: I described myself as helping her to bring forth more life-enhancing stories so she could live a good life. 'Your father was responsible for the sex abuse,' I said. 'The man who raped you was responsible for what he did against your will.' This helped her take up a less self-blaming position in relation to both contexts.

A week later Leanne told me that she had decided to report the incident to the police. This was a new storyline. When I explored how she had decided to do this she said, 'I didn't want him to get away with it.' This showed that she was taking charge of her life and we applauded this new position.

Reflexive positioning

'Reflexive positioning' is what we do when we are thinking about ourselves, privately positioning ourselves throughout the course of a day in our 'private subvocal dialogues' (Moghaddam 1999). We constantly tell ourselves stories about ourselves and, as we prepare to tell fragments of our personal accounts to others and imagine their response, various discursive positions emerge and this intentionally or unintentionally helps to position us. For example, after having been conned, a person appraises and justifies their responses; they could describe themselves as 'smart, foolish, astute or gullible, sophisticated or naive, suspicious or trusting, powerful or power-less, dominant or submissive, and so on' (Moghaddam 1999: p. 76). Working with these shifting, evolving reflexive positions is at the heart of the therapeutic process as we talk with clients, helping them tell more hopeful autobiographical stories. And reflexive therapists are also involved in reflexive positioning as we tell stories about our own abilities.

Leanne told me that when she reported the rape the woman police officer was sympathetic, which made her think that she was 'worthy' of receiving such help. I noticed that she had begun to tell more positive self-stories of being courageous. When she described herself in these fresh and more positive ways the thrill I felt enabled me to reflexively position myself as a skilful therapist.

At our next conversation, however, everything had changed again. Leanne told me that when her mother heard about the rape she'd said, 'Why do these things always happen to you?' Leanne was upset and re-connected to her previous self-blaming and self-punishing position by cutting herself again.

Her mother's reaction positioned both of us differently: in my inner self-reflections I felt unsure about how to respond and was saddened and concerned about how her mother's remark had affected Leanne.

Leanne's greatest wish was to have a good, close relationship with her mother, so these comments were a blow. Throughout her childhood and adolescence she had been cool and distant with her mother, never returning her hugs, because of how her father had positioned her in their secret life. I didn't want to simply support Leanne against her mother, as this could 'negatively connote' her mother and spoil their relationship, which was blossoming but still rather fragile.

Talking to Peter Lang in supervision he suggested that Leanne's mother's comments could be a wish for them to move on from the past. When her mother had said, 'Why do these things always happen to you?' perhaps she was asking, 'Why can't we put it all behind us? Why can't we move on? What's holding us up?'

There were at least four voices in the room: Leanne enjoyed talking to Peter through me and I enjoyed talking to her mother through her; I kept hoping that her mother could be there in person, but although Leanne was keen, her mother refused to meet me because she hadn't found previous family therapy helpful.

I wanted to understand things from her mother's position so asked Leanne, 'If your mother were here, what would she want me to know about her life?' Leanne told me how her mother had adored her charismatic father but it had become an abusive marriage and she had eventually gathered the strength to leave him. Later, finding out that he had sexually abused her first-born daughter was her worst nightmare. And now, just as she hoped that Leanne was getting her life together she'd heard that Leanne had been raped.

'Perhaps she was dreadfully upset about the rape and hoped that one day you would be living a happy, normal life, free of the effects of what your father had done to you?' I said.

I remembered that her mother had immediately believed her when she'd made the disclosure about the sex abuse and I wondered aloud what it might be like for a mother to receive yet another bombshell, particularly since Leanne had started to self-harm again. These ideas helped Leanne take a different position towards her mother; we began to notice things that demonstrated her mother's devotion and her enduring strength throughout so many tough and painful years.

Taking a risk: making a self-disclosure

Certain topics can feel risky for therapists. But Barry Mason (2005) challenges the familiar idea that we must establish trust before we take a risk:

risk-taking and trust are in a mutual relationship with each other, and if we are open with clients we can create trust, he says. His interest in risk-taking came from his own family, where they didn't take emotional risks, which hindered intimacy. 'I do not think we develop therapeutic intimacy if we play it safe. If we can take the risk of learning to challenge . . . from respectful positions, rather than just play safe, we are more likely to develop collaborative, trusting relationships' (p. 169). Of course, one therapist may be able to disclose something that would feel like a risk for another.

We develop self-reflexivity by asking ourselves what risks we are taking in terms of how we address sex, sexual orientation, race and culture, gender, religion, and disability and what themes, issues and feelings we are pulling back from.

Leanne was communicating something by self-harming, which still puzzled me. But it was spoiling her life. I decided to take a risk. 'Could you find another response to self-harming?' I asked. 'Otherwise you punish yourself twice or thrice.'

She and her mother had played it safe in their relationship; Leanne was rather 'compliant' and her mother seemed afraid to confront her, perhaps because of her own guilt that she hadn't been aware that her husband had been sexually abusing her daughter?

Then Leanne told her mother that she'd been cutting herself. For the first time in their lives they had a furious argument. I said that this could be their way of developing an ability to be open with each other, and Leanne liked this idea.

But Leanne asked herself whether it was worth taking a risk to talk more openly with her mother if it could be so upsetting? Something about this resonated for me: I made a connection with the complicated relationship I'd had with my own mother and I wondered whether it would help Leanne if I told her some of this.

It can be important to scan and identify why you think it might be useful to share a personal story and make a deliberate self-disclosure, Janine Roberts (2005) suggests. Will it help the client by offering something new? How could it affect your relationship with them, and so on?

Patrick Casement (1985), an analytic psychotherapist, uses the concept of 'trial identification'. Drawing on Wilhelm Fliess's (1942) 'internal supervisor' (which is not an internalised supervisor); trial identification helps therapists reflect on the possible effect of what we are about to say to a client. First, the therapist thinks and feels themselves into the client's description of their experience, then the therapist puts themselves into the shoes of the person the client is referring to; finally thinking about their own relationship with the client. Related to empathy, this is 'the capacity to be in two places at once, in the patient's shoes and in one's own simultaneously . . .' (Casement 1985: p. 35).

> I try to listen . . . to what . . . crosses my mind . . . silently trying out a possible comment or interpretation. This helps me to recognize when a patient could mis-hear what I wish to say, because of its ambiguity or due to an unfortunate choice of words . . . the unintentional . . . communications that a patient could read into what I have just said. Then, when I listen to the patient's subsequent response, it becomes easier to see when this has been actually provoked by me, by my timing or manner of interpreting . . . (p. 34)

In my imagination I played with what to say and how Leanne might respond. I decided to take a risk, hoping she would enjoy hearing about my own experiences. In a tentative way, I said, 'I had a tricky relationship with my mother.'

She looked interested and asked me to go on. I decided to tell her a funny story about how I'd hurt my mother by calling her 'crazy'. It was a 'trendy' saying at the time, but my mother didn't realise and took it literally.

Leanne laughed and I could tell that she enjoyed my self-disclosure. I went on to say that I hadn't appreciated how well my mother had coped with being a lone parent in a foreign country. I said that since my mother had died I'd had enduring regrets that I hadn't told her how much I valued her, although I probably had demonstrated this in practical ways. Therapy had helped me improve my relationship with her but I still regretted not expressing my appreciation for her life-long devotion and hard work, directly in words. I made sure that I kept the focus on Leanne and her relationship with her mother, making it clear why I was telling these stories.

As it felt quite risky I asked Leanne how hearing this had affected her. She said she was grateful to me and felt 'reassured'; a previous therapist had been supportive, but because she seemed to live a charmed life this reiterated Leanne's sense of being 'bad' and 'different' from the rest of humanity. My self-disclosure had helped her feel more 'normal'.

In the research Janine Roberts (2005) refers to, clients invariably spoke of instances when their therapist had shared something about their personal struggles, when they were asked what they found most helpful in therapy. They said things like, 'Those stories helped me to see that we're all human' and 'I wasn't a bad person', 'I felt less alone' and 'I learned how we are all vulnerable' (p. 53).

When we offer something of our own experience it is important to be tentative, to present a small piece of information about our experience then check out the client's responses. Janine Roberts's tentative disclosure about her own experience of breast cancer to a woman who'd just been diagnosed with cancer led to a discussion about whether to tell the children, which formed a vital part of the work.

However, it is important to consider where the disclosure might take us emotionally, she says, so we can stay emotionally present and focused on the feelings and thoughts of the clients. Also, more importantly, when we make a personal disclosure it is useful to talk about what it was like to grapple with a dilemma, rather than present it as something we have solved (p. 56). If we present a dilemma that we have solved this could make us appear rather smug and could put the client into a 'failure' position.

I had presented my disclosure as a personal regret, showing Leanne that I had understood her reluctance to talk to her mother. Now I explored the effect of the argument she'd had with her mother and was surprised and pleased when she said it had helped them feel closer. 'Maybe it shows that you both yearn for a better relationship with each other?' I suggested.

At the end of the conversation I asked Leanne what had been most helpful and she said that hearing about my relationship with my mother had been extremely useful and enjoyable. She felt less of a failure. My risk had 'worked'.

The effects of self-disclosure on client's relationships

It is important to think about how a deliberate self-disclosure might affect other people, in terms of 'joining, alliances, and coalitions' (Roberts 2005: p. 57).

I had been including Leanne's mother and their relationship throughout our conversations, creating a three-way conversation, sometimes taking Leanne's position, sometimes deliberately taking her mother's. My own personal experiences had given me a particular sensitivity to the powerful love that can underpin a mother–daughter relationship. Shifting back and forth between the different positions enabled Leanne to take different positions.

Over time, Leanne's relationship with her mother began to improve. I was delighted when Leanne announced that her mother, who lived in another town, would be coming to London and would like to meet me. This was particularly exciting because I knew that she had not enjoyed conversations with other professionals.

Before the meeting Leanne told me that she wanted to talk about how her mother's 'obsession' with death and strong fear of death affected her. This resonated for me because of my regrets, after my mother's death, about conversations I'd not had with her.

When they arrived I greeted Leanne's mother warmly and said how honoured I felt that she had come to talk with me. I asked them to let me know if the conversation was getting too intrusive, recalling that Leanne's disclosure had catapulted the family into years of distressing and shameful professional questioning.

Monica, Leanne's mother, and Leanne soon launched into a passionate conversation: Leanne explained how hurtful it was to hear her mother talk about her fear of death; Monica agreed that she was afraid to die. I said that maybe because of her deep love for her daughter she didn't want to leave before Leanne was properly 'well'.

This was a powerful turning point in the conversation: Monica cried and said that because she herself had been sexually abused by her own mother (which Leanne knew about) she'd 'never learned how to love', or 'to be a mother who can love her daughter'. Now that we had developed a good rapport I felt able to challenge these strong stories. It was quite clear, I said, from everything I'd heard, that she was obviously a devoted mother. Leanne agreed. And, even if she died tomorrow, I said, which we all hoped she wouldn't, she would have done an excellent job having laid the foundations for Leanne's future. They both liked this reformulation of their relationship.

Tears were shed by all three of us during this passionate two-hour-long conversation. Leanne told me later that this was the first meeting with a professional in which her mother had not become angry.

Deliberate self-disclosure is an influential therapeutic tool, if used with skill. However, it is important to reflect on how this could position the client and the significant people in their life. If we disclose something that shows us as having successfully resolved a dilemma this could position the client as inadequate; whereas disclosing something as a regret or unresolved shows that we are, like our client, a person travelling through life with many dilemmas.

Epilogue

Here is the email Leanne sent to me six months after she had moved back to live in her mother's town.

Hi Fran

I just wanted to send you a thank you email.

Thank you for helping me and my mum to achieve such a good relationship. I had a great day with my mum yesterday. She came with me to a meeting [this was related to a course Leanne was hoping to do]. I have never asked her to help me out in practical things. I have realised how much my mum really wants to take part in my life, being a mum and a support . . . the relationship between us has grown so much, and we are really enjoying the time we have together.

I can see that it all started to change after she came to London to talk to you. You helped me to understand how grateful I am to have my mum, and all the work and love she has for me has helped me sooooooo much!!!!

Thank you soooo much Fran. You have really done something great! I do not know how to show how much you have helped me and my mum, but I do want you to know that we are ever so grateful! You are in our thoughts every day!

Los of love

Leanne (and my mum)

Reflexive questions

- What are you accidentally disclosing through your skin colour, your clothes, your room, place of work and so on?
- Have you used deliberate self-disclosure with a client and how did they respond?
- Are you willing to be transparent about your professional approaches and theories with clients?

- Which topics and subjects do you pull back from exploring with certain clients?
- Would your clients describe you as open, or cautious about telling stories about yourself or others?
- What would you never disclose to any client, no matter what?

6

LISTENING TO OUR BODILY RESPONSES

Texts, such as this one, inevitably foreground the written, disembodied, word; but when we meet another person in our therapeutic conversations our worlds collide and intertwine in extraordinarily visceral ways.

Something exciting happened in my third meeting with Tilly and Jon which I felt in my body. In this chapter I describe how paying attention to my own bodily responses helped me listen more closely to something that was highly significant in their relationship.

American pragmatist philosopher John Dewey (1934), amongst others, contested the idea of a mind/body split. He reminds us that, like all animals, we experience and participate in the world directly through our senses and organs. Although we are different from birds and beasts, we share the same vital functions and needs: our brain coordinates our bodily senses and movements; we live *within* our environment, not merely in it, but through our interaction with it (p. 12).

There is a tendency to highlight the verbal in therapeutic work, but we interact with each other through the whole of our physical bodies, as well as through our 'minds' and the stories we tell each other. As I struggle to describe these intensely moving conversations I invite the reader to imagine the richness of the bodily aspects. I describe what John Dewey (1934) calls a 'consummatory' moment (or experience), an aesthetic moment of equilibrium, harmony and completion that comes after a time of exploration and struggle (pp. 16–18), and that is described by Vernon Cronen (Cronen and Chetro-Szivos 2002). Reflexivity involves noticing these special whole body 'moving', 'poetic' or 'living' moments in therapy (Arlene Katz and John Shotter 1996).

The heart of therapy is 'self-referencing' (Elkaim 1990). We always make a connection with what we know, what is familiar in our own life, and such 'countertransference' feelings, thoughts and ideas can create a bridge between us and the client, as long as we realise that what we have noticed is not 'reality' and that there are always multiple ways to describe everything in our social worlds.

The importance of bodily communications and responses

In every moment of a therapeutic conversation there is an enormous wealth of information, much of which is experienced non-verbally; we respond and react to another person through the intermingling of our bodies and our senses as two living, breathing, embodied beings as well as through what we say to each other. We are 'living-growing beings', '*bodily* responsive' to people and events around us; we *respond* to those around us in a direct and immediate, unthinking way with our bodies and we also affect or 'move' others in bodily ways (Shotter 2004: p. 6).

Our bodies are crucial in reflexive practices. It is no coincidence that we talk about 'gut feelings'. Intuition, imagination and perception are involved in developing new ideas, which may be sensed in our body in the same way as we become aware of a physical sensation. This could be called 'embodied knowledge' or 'somatic modes of attention' (Thomas Csordas 2002: p. 253). What often begins as an embodied sensation can be an important clue to the 'unsaid'.

When I first met Tilly I noticed that she was a white woman of medium height and her body shape could be described as 'cuddly', which endeared me to her, being less than svelte myself. She was an elegantly-dressed, cheerful woman in her mid-40s who moved confidently with an expressive, open, communicative style. She was easy to talk to, smiling and laughing readily. I liked her right away, feeling my body relax and open up in response to her.

I was calm yet alert as I 'listened' closely with my whole body to what she was communicating. When she said she'd been crying for some weeks for 'no reason' I was puzzled and felt a constriction in my throat.

She told me about her busy professional life; she was 'happily married' to Jon, who had his own IT business; they had two children, a girl aged 11 and a boy aged 14. On the surface everything in her life seemed good. She said her feelings of hopelessness and distress made her cry for several hours at a time but she didn't know why. I felt a kind of ache in my chest, a physical wave of compassion for her.

As well as feeling her sadness, I warmed to Tilly's sparky sense of humour; she responded to me by talking freely, showing that she valued being able to talk to me. I wanted to make sense of what was happening in her life right now, how her stories from the past affected how she was feeling and her hopes for the future. When I asked her what she hoped for in life she said she wanted to be happy, enjoying her work and her family. 'I don't understand,' she said, 'there's no reason for me to feel so rotten.'

'Withness' and 'aboutness' thinking

John Shotter (2004) contrasts 'aboutness' or 'monological-thinking' with 'withness' thinking. 'Aboutness' thinking seeks universal 'truths' and 'explanations' *about* people. This way of talking about people, he says, is normal in academic and intellectual lives in the West but is dehumanising (pp. i–ii). However, in 'withness' (or 'dialogical') thinking, people are uniquely responsive, embodied people, who move together in an active, jointly created 'dance': a 'social poetics'.

If I were to use 'aboutness' thinking I might be tempted to search for a theory about 'depression' to 'explain' Tilly's feelings. But I didn't want to do this. 'We don't understand – yet . . .' I replied. I wanted to convey hopefulness and explore the unique reasons for Tilly's misery, to listen with my whole body and 'move with her'. For the time being I allowed the conversation to flow, feeling the uncertainty of not knowing the 'reasons' for Tilly's hopelessness.

Then she told me that she feared the return of a 'breakdown' she'd had two years ago because she'd been wrongly accused of something at work; although she had been exonerated she was still affected by what had happened. As we talked I noticed that her breathing became a little slower and as she visibly began to relax, so did I.

Self-referencing

Self-referencing is the 'trump card' in therapy, according to Mony Elkaim (1990). Because objective truth in human relationships is not possible, none of us can be an 'objective' or 'neutral' observer; we cannot separate ourselves from any situation we describe. The 'observer' in all human relationships is always part of what is being 'observed' (von Foerster 1984;

Humberto Maturana and Francisco Varela 1987). It is not so much that we 'include' the observer, Varela (1988) says; there is no distinct entity of 'observer', since we all emerge in the process of interaction.

Each of us constructs our personal version of reality: 'Our own histories inevitably influence us when we try to describe the world' (p. xx). But rather than this self-referencing being a handicap it is an asset when we do therapy because it helps us create a special and unique bridge between us and the client.

Tilly had a strong work ethic: her parents encouraged her to be a conscientious worker. I 'noticed' this story amongst the numerous others I could have told about her because I made a self-reference to my own similar stories. My work ethic stories created a bridge between us and I told her how much I empathised with her position.

Another therapist might have identified with other themes; there are no 'correct' or 'incorrect' stories, just ones that are more, or less, useful for the client. The stories we select when we make a bridge must, of course, be based on sound ethical principles: being appreciative, hopeful, and viewing everybody as doing the best they can, given all the circumstances.

Connecting with, or not connecting with, a person's metaphor

As we came towards the end of the conversation Tilly said that her manager had suggested that she work from home sometimes. She was considering the idea. I was enthusiastic and just a little envious. Perhaps, I said, doing this would help her feel less stressed?

At our second meeting, a month later, Tilly said working from home some days had helped. But she was still crying 'for no reason' and because of the previous 'breakdown' believed she was probably 'doomed' to get 'depressed'. I felt a sense of alarm in my stomach. Although I was curious about where Tilly had developed these ideas, I was prejudiced against the 'breakdown' metaphor, which seems more applicable to a machine than to a complex human person, and this made me not want to expand these themes.

In our culture, 'depression' is a catch-all term describing a wide variety of emotions. But it is problematic and comes from a disease/medical model, claims psychiatrist Paul Keedwell (2008), and this is 'preventing a more complete understanding of why we as a species are so susceptible to depression'. The idea that one will experience frequent 'bouts' or 'episodes' of something as complex as depression *for no reason* can feel like a life sentence. And when therapists reify 'depression' (turn 'it' into a thing) and try to *explain* a 'phenomenon', they are using what John Shotter would call 'aboutness', or 'monological thinking'.

I preferred to use 'withness thinking' to explore the unique aspects of Tilly's stories, the particular contexts and relationships in which she was experiencing certain feelings. Since nothing had changed since our last meeting I guessed that there must be some meaning that Tilly and I had not yet noticed, some relationship and some communication we hadn't yet explored. I recalled the year-long period of sick leave she had taken following the work-related conflict.

'How did Jon respond, when you were off work that time?' I asked.

'He was great, so kind and helpful,' Tilly said, and described many ways he had been supportive. This, I thought, showed that they had a strong marriage.

Her expression was bright; she waved her hands about in an energetic way describing an ability to juggle the competing demands of being a wife, mother and professional woman easily and expertly. I said I was impressed with the way she handled everything well. I was connecting to a familiar idea that women often put others' interests before their own.

When I offered these ideas Tilly agreed, but added that she and Jon shared some of the domestic chores and anyway these practical things came easily to her. 'So why do I feel so miserable?' she asked. And tears came into her eyes.

Therapists' bodily responses help them notice something different

Somehow what she was saying and what she was doing (as in laughing or crying) did not quite match; I felt a sense of discomfort in my body. Was I missing something? Perhaps I was observing the 'wrong' things or not asking the right kind of questions?

I was puzzled by how often Tilly smiled and laughed, then just as quickly began to cry. Because of this rapid shift in mood it was difficult for me to 'notice' the specific times when she became distressed.

As I was puzzling about this, Tilly said Jon was a man with many interests. 'He's just as much of a workaholic as I am,' she laughed. 'He's always so busy, always working. I wish he would spend more time with me.' I felt my body become more alert at hearing this new information.

'The important things in life do not simply occur in the person's mind, but in their whole body, their whole being,' says family therapist Tom Andersen (1992: p. 55). 'As I am open and sensitive to what I see, hear, feel, taste, and smell, I can also notice "answers" to those touches from myself, as my body, "from inside", lets me know in various ways how it thinks about what the outside touches; what should be concentrated on and what not' (p. 55). He was inspired by physiotherapist Aadel Bulow-Hansen, who worked with breathing and bodily responses and this helped him notice the small, almost imperceptible ways his body responded to clients' stories. When we listen closely, following the client, not only do we hear the words but we also see *how* the words are uttered, noticing that every word is part of the moving of the body (Andersen 1993).

'What would you like to do more of with Jon?' I asked.

'Just go for a walk like we used to,' she said, with a short laugh, waving her hand in a dismissive way. Perhaps she was 'saying' that surely it was not such a big thing to go for a walk with your husband occasionally?

'What kinds of things did you enjoy doing together?' I asked.

'All the normal things,' she answered. In the early days of their relationship she and Jon would go to the cinema, the theatre or out for meals. And they used to have fun days out as a family, but now that the children were older and had their own interests these family outings had dwindled.

'He doesn't seem to want to do anything with me any more.' Her face became pink and tears welled up in her eyes.

I felt my body tighten and my breathing become shallow. I became alert: something extremely important was happening. Although Tilly often cried, perhaps this time I was making a proper connection between what she was 'saying' verbally and what she was 'saying' with her body?

My body was 'touched' by Tilly's words and her tears. It came to me suddenly that Jon was the one person who could help us understand things differently. It was not that I thought he had 'caused' her unhappiness or that there was a 'lack' in their relationship, just that maybe they were more connected than was obvious.

'Would Jon be willing to join us?' I asked casually, with a sense of anticipation.

'He doesn't like talking about feelings,' Tilly replied.

'Perhaps he might come if he thought it would help you?'

She said she would ask him, but wasn't hopeful.

Bodies are socially and culturally constituted

I was surprised and delighted when Jon arrived with Tilly for the next meeting, and felt a buzz of excitement. Right away I noticed his height and size; he seemed to fill the small waiting area. His height and bulk gave him gravitas and he smiled in a genial way. His large body, when he sat down, more than filled the chair.

As Chris Shilling (2003) points out, as well as being composed of bones, muscles, flesh and blood, our bodies are *socially constituted*: they serve as social symbols and give an indication of where we are positioned socially and culturally. Through our bodies we act on the world and they are the vehicle through which we come to experience the world.

In therapy we 'must go beyond cognition and language', Rabia Malik and Inga-Britt Krause (2005) say, 'there is scope for developing a whole repertoire of using ourselves, what we wear and how, how we sit and stand, how we interact with our clients'. In their fascinating examples of dilemmas involving touch, gifts, imagery and clothing, they describe a male therapist who didn't realise that a Muslim woman is not permitted to touch a man who is not her husband. The therapist, from his cultural position, showed politeness by shaking the hand of the Muslim woman interpreter. Although the team reprimanded him behind the screen, he went on to do a sensitive interview. At the end the mother of the family, a traditional woman, got up, walked over to the therapist, took his hand and shook it. Her daughters followed her example. The mother had returned the therapist's greeting with her body, repeating his gesture of openness and intimacy in a remarkable contradiction of her cultural norms (pp. 101–2).

Gender is often the first distinction people make when they meet someone. I'd felt comfortable with Tilly and was less immediately comfortable with Jon. He was a man and, as such, was for me 'the other'. However, his casual clothes and broad, smiling face made him feel less of an imposing presence.

I welcomed him and thanked him for coming, aware that he'd not been keen to come initially and he might be entering 'alien territory'. My preference is to make therapeutic conversations as relaxed as possible and I wanted the process to feel easy for Jon. This could also help us discuss more challenging themes if and when the time came.

In answer to my question about what each of them were hoping for from the conversation Jon said he wanted to help Tilly feel better. She agreed. I explored what they appreciated about each other and what their relationship meant for them; Tilly talked about practical aspects: Jon shared jobs around the house and she enjoyed spending time with him. Jon used more abstract terms such as 'loyalty'.

Self-referencing continued . . .

The concept of self-referencing shows us that it is entirely normal for therapists to make connections with our own lives. Indeed, 'it is not possible to speak of a human relationship as if the observer were not part of the situation being described' (Elkaim 1990: p. xx). The solution, he says, is not to try to avoid self-reference but to use it as the heart of the therapy (p. 170). First we listen to what arises inside us; our stories, thoughts, feelings and bodily reactions provide invaluable clues to what is happening with the client.

> In general the first thing that comes to your mind is very important because it shows you the unique bridge between the others and yourself; but at the same time you run the risk, if you follow it as you experience it, of confirming your own world view and the client's, which does not help either of us to change. The first feeling could be the most obvious, it could relate more to our own stories, which could reiterate the client's stories and create more of the same.   (pp. 171–2)

So, 'rule number two', he says, is to be sceptical. However, if the feeling fits with the client as well as ourselves, then we will have discovered a 'special and unique bridge' between the client and ourselves.

Eventually Tilly began talking about her wish that Jon would spend more time with her. He described how his business and many activities kept him busy. I felt a kind of agitation in my body that was alerting me to something. Had the marriage taken a back seat? Was Jon taking her for granted? Perhaps they had different priorities. Were there gender differences? Had

Jon's numerous interests and commitments taken over? Was work more important for Jon than spending time with Tilly?

I was making a self-reference to a gender story: some men focus on work to the exclusion of their family. The feelings linked with this idea were a kind of annoyance with Jon but I wanted to get out of the story that Jon was a man who was reluctant, or 'too busy', to spend time with his partner; obviously something that had been co-created by me and Tilly and Jon in our conversations. So I began to explore the enjoyable things they used to do together. Jon agreed that they enjoyed going to see films, plays and going to restaurants and didn't know why they'd stopped doing this. By the end of the meeting he had agreed to do more social things with Tilly.

However, at the second meeting a month later, they said that apart from going on an enjoyable walk, nothing had changed. Jon said he was simply 'too busy'.

I was puzzled and felt a frisson of 'frustration' in my body and a tightening in my jaw at hearing this familiar story. I sympathised more with Tilly and her wish to spend time with Jon and was less sympathetic to Jon's explanations about his busy schedule. We spent time exploring their hopes for the relationship and the family.

At our third meeting Jon said almost immediately 'I'm being a pain.'

Everything in my body became alert. I was surprised that Jon had initiated the conversation. He gave a short laugh and shifted his bulky frame in the chair. He'd found talking about himself challenging and he often said Tilly could 'run rings round him' as far as talking about feelings was concerned. This was something different.

I noticed the intense way he had said the words and his large motionless body. Tilly looked solemn. She, too, sat still looking at Jon with serious attentiveness. I noticed that I was holding my breath: it felt like an important moment.

Words 'touch' us

I wanted to reconnect with Jon's powerful statement that he was being 'a pain', which he had blurted out with such awkwardness. I guessed that he had taken a risk and also wondered what it meant that he had initiated the conversation.

'In what way are you being 'a pain'?' I asked.

'I'm being a pain – as far as Tilly's concerned,' he said.

Again he shifted uncomfortably in his seat.

I flinched at the word 'pain'. But because I was curious about the effect it was having on both of them I began to explore his meanings. Usually I wouldn't want to expand such a potentially damaging description, but it seemed important to do so.

As he began to speak, Tilly answered. *'What he means is that I want us to spend more time together.'*

It was the familiar story. But now, because of Jon's statement I began to pay more attention.

'When do you feel this longing most?' I asked Tilly.

'In the evening,' she answered. She explained that she would cook and then the family would eat a meal together. Then Jon would go into his study to work, reappearing to watch the ten-o'clock news but often falling asleep in front of the television. Then he'd return to his study until the early hours of the morning, by which time Tilly would have gone to bed and be asleep.

Was Tilly talking about a possible lack of sexual intimacy? Before I could explore this she said quite angrily to Jon, *'You're always working. Your work spills over into everything. If I've got a job to do I'll get on with it, get it finished.'*

I had heard this before. But now I was literally sitting up, taking notice with my whole being.

'Yes, but it'll have mistakes in it,' Jon said forcefully, *'I want to get my reports absolutely right and this takes time.'*

I wondered whether Jon was less easy-going than he appeared. And was this 'perfectionism' an indication that he was worried about his business?

'I'm wondering,' I said, *'whether you're concerned about maintaining your client-base?'* I imagined a competitive field populated by young thrusting types who were poised to snatch his business away from him.

'No,' he said, firmly.

I was a bit surprised. Where had I got the idea that the business was precarious? I knew some people in the IT world but this self-reference didn't fit for Jon.

Although Jon didn't agree with me at the time, six months later with the downturn in the economy he did in fact lose a large chunk of his business. I had connected to something that Jon wasn't willing to acknowledge at the time because of his strong desire to be the one who was supporting his family, as he told me later.

'In any case,' Tilly said, 'he's not always working when he's in the study.'

'What else are you doing?' I asked him.

'The family's accounts,' Tilly said, adding that she appreciated him doing them.

'But,' she said to him, 'sometimes you're sitting at the computer dozing. I've been tempted to take a video of you so you can see yourself.' And she laughed. Jon also gave a short laugh, looking straight ahead; his face was in profile and I couldn't see his expression.

'Perhaps, you're actually tired,' I suggested, 'which is why you're dozing in front of the computer?' I had calculated that he normally got only five or six hours' sleep and by saying this was making a self-reference; I would not have been able to function with so little sleep.

Jon agreed and I began to be uncomfortably aware that we seemed to be focusing on his shortcomings.

To shift the focus from this I was reminded of Badger in the children's book Wind in the Willows. Did they know the book? I asked. Luckily they did. 'Remember Badger, who would go into his study to "work", but it was well-known that he would be sleeping (hibernating for the winter),' I said. We all laughed.

By connecting with this couple's humorous style I avoided 'negatively connoting' Jon as 'the one with the problem' and also showed Tilly that I appreciated her position.

Getting 'outside' a story that 'bewitches' us

However, as the conversation continued I became more and more puzzled by the circularity of the themes. The story that we were co-constructing was of a reluctant husband who refused, for whatever reason, to spend time with his wife. I assumed that Jon was happy with the amount of time they spent together because he had not said otherwise.

When we are listening to somebody, Elsbeth McAdam and Peter Lang (2006) say, we become bewitched by the way the story is told, drawing on

Wittgenstein's (1953) observation that our language bewitches us. By language we include all kinds of bodily ways of communicating. McAdam and Lang describe how, as you are becoming bewitched you get more and more caught up in that story. 'If you want to create something, simply look in the places where you wouldn't normally look. Look around. Get outside the story' (p. 84).

When I looked at Jon's large soft body it seemed to be 'speaking' to me: was he 'comfort-eating' and what did this mean? Could this relate to him feeling bad about himself or disappointed with life, or something else?

I began to explore other ideas: was Jon reluctant to go out per se?

'No!' he said; he went out to visit his clients and attend meetings at his various clubs. He just didn't seem to be keen on going out for pleasure, particularly with Tilly.

I'd felt my frustration with him as a tightness in my chest and I wanted to cut through the circularity. Was this a similar frustration that Tilly felt?

Before I realised what I was doing, I turned to Jon and said, 'So, the marriage isn't so important to you?'

Harry Goolishian was reputed to have said, 'we don't know what we think until we say it – when we talk we find out what we are thinking' (John Shotter 2007).

'Of course my marriage is important to me,' Jon said almost angrily, 'it's my main priority in life.' I was taken aback by the strength of his reaction.

I hadn't realised that I'd wanted Jon to confirm his commitment to the marriage until I'd asked that question. I thanked him; it was useful to hear him say that so clearly. His powerful reply had helped me get 'outside' the story that he was a reluctant partner. And by the keen way she watched and listened, Tilly seemed to like his response.

But I still felt uneasy; there was a tension in my stomach; something didn't fit. I recalled that Jon had told me that his father had high hopes for him to be successful. These hopes weren't properly formulated and he'd constantly criticised Jon, who never knew how to please his father.

'Is there any connection with your father's high expectations of you and what's going on between you and Tilly?' I asked him.

'You're going down the right tunnel,' he said, thoughtfully, turning to look at me, 'but you're not there yet.' His glasses gleamed and I couldn't see his eyes.

'Success, for Jon's father, means being married with children,' Tilly said. This surprised me. I had viewed success in business and financial terms.

Another story flickered on the edge of my consciousness: Jon's mother, who had died some time ago, had wanted him to be a girl. She'd been bitterly disappointed all her life that Jon was a boy. Both parents had seemed to be disappointed with him. Was this important, and in what way?

Our bodily responses are clues to the 'unsaid'

Now Tilly began talking about the times when Jon came back from the supermarket. 'If he comes back with the wrong kind of cereal or forgets something he gets in a state,' she said.

'What does he do when he's in a state?' I asked Tilly.

'He'll hit out at something; he even hits his head against the wall,' she answered.

'It doesn't hurt,' Jon laughed, although this time his joking seemed rather strained.

I was holding my breath and experienced a tightening in my stomach, a sick feeling.

The way Jon shrugged off his self-harming with a laugh made me feel apprehensive; something crucial that had been 'unsaid' was beginning to be talked about. Tilly told me about many other times when Jon would hurt himself if he had got something wrong; I noticed his bodily stillness. The atmosphere in that tiny room was intense.

'Why do you think he does that?' I asked Tilly, keeping an eye on Jon.

'He's angry with himself' she replied. Jon was in profile to me, so I couldn't see his face properly. He looked directly at Tilly, not smiling, not speaking. I felt my stomach lurch.

'Transference' and 'countertransference' is the tip of something much larger

Transference refers to the client's reactions and feelings towards the therapist. 'Transference is simple; people treat us in a particular way and we come to expect people to treat us in that way,' John Bowlby says (Lang 2008).

Transference in human relations, according to Gregory Bateson (1979), is general, universal and normal. We think in stories and our learning happens within sequences of experiences with important others in our lives; our experiences are built into our very being, and patterns of childhood experience are built into us:

> my father did so and so; my aunt did such and such; and what they did was outside my skin . . . [and] the shape of what happened between you and me yesterday carries over to shape how we respond to each other today. And that shaping is . . . a *transference* from past learning. (p. 24)

'Countertransference' refers to the therapist's reactions and feelings towards the client. 'The meaning and function of the therapist's feelings in the context of the therapeutic system are the tools both for understanding the system and for intervening in it' (Elkaim 1990).

My thoughts, feelings and bodily responses drawn from numerous personal and professional experiences were alerting me to something important. Then Jon turned to look at me, his large, soft body immobile. As my stomach lurched again I felt a whoosh of empathy for him.

Here was a man who was so angry with himself that he harmed himself. Something about the way he sat silently, something about him being a disappointment to both his parents, and now to Tilly, evoked empathy in me.

For the first time I felt a strong and deep connection with Jon and his stories of being criticised.

'What the therapist feels relates not only to his or her personal history but also to the system in which the feelings emerge,' Mony Elkaim says. 'What we call transference and countertransference, is only the tip of a much larger iceberg.' Complex elements come into play at the 'intersection' between the therapist and the client (or couple, or family): our personal histories, professional stories, our morals and values, the context in which we work and the numerous voices that are influencing us.

Therapists' countertransference can involve connections to personal stories related to gender, ethnicity, colour, class, age, differing abilities and so on. Something in the client's story will 'resonate' with one or more of our own stories to co-create something that exists in this intersection that 'belongs' to both of us.

Countertransference can involve the voices of important others in the life of the therapist including other colleagues, the voice of our supervisor, the context in which the therapy takes place, including the institution if we work in one; it is not just related to the client.

I sensed that Jon was a man who was groping towards something, as I too was groping towards something. The way his glasses gleamed had made it difficult to see his eyes; I now realised that when he 'looked' at me his eyes were closed. Perhaps he didn't want me to 'see' him. Maybe he did this in the way that a child closes their eyes when they want to hide? No wonder it was hard to 'read' him. He had been 'hiding' in his office, perhaps he didn't want anyone to 'see' him? What was Jon hiding, or what was he hiding from? Or, to reframe this idea: what was he protecting himself from?

Maybe Jon had wanted to 'hide' from possible criticism, in his office and inside his work. Maybe his numerous interests maintained his commitment to his wife and children, yet enabled him to protect himself in some way.

We all waited. Nobody moved and nobody said anything. I felt a lump in my throat and a great sense of compassion for him. I remembered that he'd said at the beginning of the conversation, 'I'm being a pain – as far as Tilly is concerned.' Maybe, his attempt to hide, to protect himself, had created the very disappointment that he had sought to avoid?

I made a self-reference to the many times when I'd felt criticised and under-valued.

This and the bodily feelings I'd had when I heard about Jon's anger towards himself, helped me make a connection with him.

I still felt a connection with Tilly, but now I felt an equally strong connection with Jon. It felt like an important moment. 'She can run rings round me with words,' Jon had said. Was he out of his depth in the emotional waters in which Tilly and I felt comfortable? He showed his distress in his actions against himself, and these were a communication to Tilly, to himself, to his children and now to me. Something like sorrow rose up into my chest and throat; it could be called a softening of my heart.

Jon, I now realised, was not a man who could shrug things off, who wasn't affected by things.

'Touching' and 'big' words provide 'openings'

'I'm guessing that you're a very sensitive man,' I said to him.

The new word 'sensitive' was a different way of describing him. He nodded in a thoughtful way, looking away from me into the middle distance. He didn't smile or make a funny comment. I guessed the word had touched him in some way.

Tom Andersen (1996) says that 'various spoken words "touch" the speaker differently. . . . It is these special, "touching" words, or "big" words – which can "touch" both those who hear them as well as those who utter them that can . . . provide "openings" into another person's "world", into the things that matter to them' (p. 21, in Shotter 2007: p. 7).

Why hadn't I explored the details of their interactions? Perhaps my empathy for Tilly's position and stories had 'bewitched' me?

Now I asked Tilly, 'When you're hurt, upset about Jon working so much, what do you do, what do you say to him?'

'Oh, I'm quite nasty,' she said openly, 'I shout and call him names.'

Again, Jon tried to brush it off with a joke. But this time I was beginning to understand the pattern.

'I'm wondering,' I said to him, 'since you're so sensitive, whether it hurts when Tilly shouts at you?' He nodded.

'Maybe it's so hurtful that, even though you love her and you live for your marriage and the children and although you'd love to spend time with her, maybe you feel so hurt by the things she says and how she says them that you want to protect yourself, hide away in your study, your cubby-hole?' Cubby-hole was the term Tilly had given for his study.

'Yes,' Jon said, 'I think you've got it . . . that's it . . . that's what it is . . .'

I felt a tremendous rush of excitement.

Being *moved* emotionally and bodily in the joint dance of a therapeutic conversation is what Arlene Katz and John Shotter (1996) call an 'arresting', 'moving', 'poetic' or 'living' moment.

113

During my many conversations with them I first connected with Tilly's feelings of distress and her frustration and disappointment with Jon, accepting that he was satisfied with things. Paying attention to my own bodily responses helped me notice his stories.

I turned to Tilly and had a short and moving conversation with her. 'It can't have been easy for him,' I said, 'growing up with his father's high expectations and his mother's disappointment that he was a boy, instead of the daughter she wanted.' Tilly agreed.

This respectful way of talking enabled her to take a different position towards Jon and her own actions; there was no need to restate the hurtful way she often spoke to him. It also gave Jon the opportunity to hear some different, more appreciative things; it was a helpful antidote.

The three of us sat in a thoughtful silence for a few moments. There was a sense of completeness, of consummation; we had made enough connections for the time being.

As John Dewey (1934) says, 'The consummatory phase of experience . . . always presents something new' (p. 144). Each step in the process leads towards this summing up and fulfilment. 'The time of consummation is also one of beginning anew' (p. 16).

There seemed to be a 'resolution', a satisfying coming together, a culmination of everything we had discussed in our previous conversations and an opening for something new.

Suddenly Jon said, 'Did we tell you, she was a divorced woman when I married her?'

'Yes, I was married before I married Jon,' Tilly said, 'It was a total mistake.'

Tripping over each other to tell the story of their relationship and finishing each others' sentences, they told me that Tilly had married a friend of Jon's but the marriage was not a success. It had lasted barely a year.

The atmosphere in the room had changed dramatically. It was light and celebratory. The laughter was free-flowing. She and Jon had always been friends, they said. Jon had even been an usher at her first wedding. Tilly had realised at the time how much she liked him. And, although he liked her too, he'd put his own wishes aside because he didn't want to spoil her happiness.

When her marriage ran into difficulties Tilly had naturally turned to Jon. But his mother was against him marrying a divorced woman; 'she was worried about what the neighbours would say,' Tilly said. But Jon had stood up for his choice of wife.

I felt a sense of relief at the joyful atmosphere in the room and joined Jon and Tilly's laughter. There was no mistaking their shared delight at having found each other. We agreed that it was a story worthy of Mills and Boon, and ended the conversation with more laughter and an appointment for a month's time. They offered profuse thanks as they left.

Tilly and Jon faced many more challenges but this conversation proved to be the turning point in their relationship. And, as Tilly said in a thank you letter she wrote much later: 'We're pulling together now, instead of pulling against each other.'

Reflexive questions

When you are in a conversation with a client:

- Notice the taste, smell and feel of everything.
- What effect do the 'big' words have on both of you?
- In what way are your bodily responses clues to the 'unsaid'?
- Do you notice countertransference responses that come from stories that are not related to the client?
- Are you willing to use self-reference to create a bridge between you and your client?
- What makes this therapeutic for the client (or not)?

7

PUTTING IT INTO PRACTICE: FURTHER IDEAS AND RESOURCES

In this chapter I discuss how a range of creative approaches can help therapists extend reflexive practices.
The practical and creative approaches I explore include:

■ developing a good context for therapy;
■ self–other-reflexivity;
■ noticing our resources;
■ relational reflexivity;
■ systemic empathy;
■ empathic imagination.

Reflexivity involves valuing our own resources as well as being willing to leave our own safe position for the time being. To paraphrase John Donne (1624), no person is an island and we develop systemic empathy as we imaginatively 'talk with' the important others in the client's life. If we invite clients into self–other-reflexive conversations we will appreciate things from every relevant position and imaginatively shift between all these positions.

This may put us in the 'dis-comfort zone', family therapist Jim Wilson (2007) says, but it is important to have the courage to extend our 'performances of practice' because using our methods too rigidly can limit more creative practices (p. 26).

Creating a good context for therapy

When I was out of the office one afternoon Marianne, our admin receptionist, rang me to say that a large, angry man had been brought into the

Counselling Service by his manager. Marianne described the scene to me on the phone: a burly security officer in his early sixties, dressed in his navy blue uniform, his face contorted with rage dominated the tiny office. He had yelled, 'If I don't get help, I don't know what I'll do.'

Apparently the man, Vince, had sworn at someone that morning, his manager said before leaving. Despite being on her own and frightened by Vince's size, angry words and threatening demeanour, Marianne heard what sounded like desperation in his voice and responded in a kindly way, saying that someone would ring him later. Vince thanked her and left. The way she described him made me curious about this man, who was not a typical client.

Reception and front line staff are rarely given credit for the way they create a context for therapy; they are in a primary position to enhance or damage the reputation of therapy services.

I told Marianne that I admired her ability to defuse a potentially dangerous situation and respond in a way that made Vince feel respected, and he said later that her response had created a good impression about the service. This created a good context for my later conversation with him.

There are many powerful discourses about 'dangerous' men in our culture. Men who speak in belligerent ways are feared, since there is an assumption that they can become violent. In our culture men tend not to seek therapeutic help, particularly working-class men, and it is thought that they don't want to talk about their feelings. But this is not necessarily the case (Lutz 1996).

Practitioners can become so caught up in our idea of help that we can fail to check whether this fits with what the client wants. Someone could want practical or financial assistance or advice, or they may want help to get another person to change.

Vince was a large, white working-class man with a forceful manner. That he had asked for 'help' made me feel hopeful. But, I wondered, did 'help' mean that he wanted to talk? He didn't fit the picture of someone who voluntarily seeks therapy. Did Vince's manager see Vince as a 'problem' he wanted someone else to 'solve'? As a woman I was aware of the social and cultural stories about unpredictable, potentially violent men, yet I wanted to question these 'taken for granted', 'common-sense' stories. Another woman therapist, perhaps someone with different stories from mine, might not have been willing to meet a man like Vince on her own.

Stories of class, gender and age are influential: in our culture younger people tend to accept the idea of talking therapies; older people may say one should 'just get on with things' and may not want to 'burden' others with their problems.

Numerous influences from wider cultural and societal contexts will have a bearing on the way we approach someone who seeks 'help': the acronym 'the GRRAACCCES' (John Burnham 1993; Roper-Hall 1997) keeps in mind stories related to gender, race, religion, age, (differing) abilities, class, colour, culture, ethnicity and sexual orientation.

Vince was white; if he had been black he might have been perceived differently since non-white people are viewed as more dangerous than white people, even by mental health professionals and even if they exhibit the same behaviour (Suman Fernando 1991: pp. 120–2). Of course no practitioner should work in contexts that pose a personal threat.

Although I was apprehensive my curiosity about this unusual person made me want to meet him. Were my instincts 'right' or was I foolhardy? Which personal resources did I draw on in making this decision?

When I rang Vince later that day I carried these questions, apprehensions, excitement and uncertainties into the conversation. But when he answered the phone he sounded nothing like the raging bull of a man I'd expected. And when I offered him an appointment for the following day he thanked me and seemed more willing than reluctant. I began to look forward to our meeting.

Self–other-reflexivity

Self–other-reflexivity, Peter Lang (2008) says, acknowledges that everything we do and say is simultaneously a communication and an invitation, an ongoing, to-and-fro communication process of responding to another person's invitations and issuing invitations to them. Our self-identities and self-descriptions emerge in this ongoing, never-ending, interweaving process of co-creation (Bakhtin 1993; Ricoeur 1972; Vygotsky 1986). Since we create our 'identities' in our conversations with other people, Peter Lang (2008) has coined the term 'we-dentity'. In therapeutic conversations self–other-reflexive therapists will, at every moment of the conversation, scan our reactions to the client and empathically scan the other person's responses to check the kinds of identities we are co-creating.

When Vince was brought into our reception his manager implicitly described him as 'a problem'. Vince's use of the word 'help' and his tone and manner made Marianne hear 'desperation' in his voice. Her personal and professional stories included a desire to help another person in distress and she 'heard' Vince's 'desperate' request as an invitation. She offered to ring me right away, knowing that my personal and professional stories included wanting to respond to a person who asked for 'help', particularly less conventional clients.

As Vince, Marianne and I responded to each other, we were issuing invitations to each other and co-constructing our self-identities together.

Vince told me later that after talking to Marianne he felt a lot better about himself, more hopeful. And, after I had rung him, he felt that at last he was going to get the 'help' that he'd been asking for. I was happy to be able to offer him this service. Marianne in turn told me that she felt good because she had been able to do something to help another person. All three of us developed good stories about ourselves. I am sure the reader can recall, as I can, times when interactions with other professionals have led to a less happy outcome.

Noticing our resources

When we enter into a new relationship with a client we draw on the multiple resources from our unique life experiences, abilities and histories. All these can be used as resources in therapy. For example, hypnotherapist Milton Erikson (Sidney Rosen 1982) developed his extraordinary observational skills when he contracted polio as a young man. He was totally paralysed, quarantined on a farm with his parents, seven sisters, a brother and a nurse.

> I got very lonesome lying in bed, unable to move anything except my eye-balls. And how could I entertain myself? I started watching people and my environment. I soon learned that my sisters could say 'no' when they meant 'yes'. And they could say 'yes' and mean 'no' at the same time. They could offer another sister an apple and hold it back. And I began studying nonverbal language and body language.   (Rosen 1982: p. 47)

Milton Erikson's remarkable ability to develop rapport with clients is evident in the inspirational 'teaching tales' that he told as he trained therapists (Jay Hayley 1973).

When Vince arrived on time for his appointment my first impression as he sat in the small waiting area was of an imposing presence. He was a big man in his mid-60s; his shaved head made him look tough. He looked as if he'd had a hard life. I noticed his polite smile and his neat, casual clothes. His deferential manner, as he followed me into the therapy room, seemed to be a kind of 'old-fashioned' chivalry. Was this respect for me as a professional or for me as a mature woman?

Vince sat on the edge of the chair and leaned forward. In that tiny room we were almost touching. Even as I was taking the practical details he started to tell me about the incident the previous morning when he had sworn at a visitor. This was not the first time he'd burst out in anger at work, he said. But he'd been undervalued by his managers at work for years. Like a river bursting its banks, the words gushed out as he described these injustices. He could be suspended; it wasn't fair; he had many debts and was afraid that he could lose his job.

I connected in a personal way with Vince's money worries. I knew that security officers are paid very little, yet Vince did not complain about this; perhaps he didn't expect to earn more.

As he spoke, Vince stabbed the air with his hands to emphasise his words and swore freely, then apologised. I waved away his apology, smiling. I was not offended by such 'colourful' language. Another therapist could have felt threatened. What was helping me see past his angry façade?

We all have unique resources, says Sheila McNamee (in Carla Guannes and Emerson Rasera 2006), which we sometimes overlook unless they are pointed out to us. For example, when she was struggling to develop therapeutic skills, someone suggested that she pretend to be a researcher, which enabled her to ask the client more useful questions (p. 132). If we are not sure what our unique resources might be we can ask clients, colleagues, friends and family members.

A fleeting thought came to me: was Vince a man who was in distress, as well as one who was angry? Maybe his passionate style was his way of trying to help me understand him and his life? When I listened to Vince the 'voices' of other men joined in: ex-offenders, homeless men and men with a mental health diagnosis. In previous jobs I'd been privileged to have talked with some of the most feared and least understood people in our society. Some of them could certainly be described as 'threatening', yet they had told me of feeling scared and unhappy, out of their depth emotionally and lacking in power. They had helped me develop the resources to heed the untold stories in what Vince was saying.

'I'm not sure whether you know this,' I said, 'but not many men come to counselling; you're pretty unusual.'

I was connecting to research and anecdotal experience that shows that women dominate therapeutic services, and wanted him to hear my appreciation of his wish to seek 'help'.

Vince smiled briefly. He went on to tell me that he'd been a bus driver for years, a job he'd loved, but had to give up because of ill-health. Working as a security officer was not as satisfying, but he enjoyed it. And now his job could be on the line. I recognised a person for whom the identity of being a working person was important; taking a pride in his work, being a conscientious and loyal employee and feeling appreciated were as important to him as the money.

Now he told me that he'd sustained a head injury in the line of duty when he confronted some trespassers at work nearly two years before, and this explained his irritability and forgetfulness. 'It's unfair,' he said. He also had numerous other health problems, which made life difficult.

In *The Shared Experience of Illness*, therapists working in medical contexts write about how their own experiences of illness influenced the way they worked with particular patients and their families (Susan McDaniel et al. 1997). The management of emotional pain is examined in therapy, 'but the management of physical pain is not'. There is an 'exclusive focus on the psychosocial world [and] most therapists are not trained to examine how their own experiences with biologically based illness shape their lives and their relationships with patients . . .' (p. 2). These experiences became personal resources that enhanced their sensitivity and enabled them to increase their empathy towards their patients. These moving stories of family illness show the universality of human struggles that can make therapists more human.

At the time, I did not pay enough attention to Vince's physical ailments, although I did note that irritability is a well-known sign of stress, drawing on my professional knowledge about the topic (Robert Sapolksy 1998) and the numerous stress awareness workshops I'd run with members of staff. At this stage it was not appropriate to self-disclose my own experiences of work-related stress, although when I did so later he found it useful.

As Vince continued with his numerous stories, which ranged over his difficult childhood and the sixty-odd years of his life, I was unsure how best to join him, which themes to explore and whether to interrupt the flow. Then he began talking in a none-too-complimentary way about his three ex-wives.

As a woman I had an unpleasant reaction, which proved to be a resource. Vince's flirtatious style helped Heleni, my co-worker, and I create a good connection with him, enabling us to confront some of Vince's strong stories about women in a humorous way. Humour was another resource that came to our aid many times in our conversations with Vince and he later said it helped him to trust us.

Relational reflexivity

Therapists may wonder how clients are experiencing the conversation, but often do not ask them to give us feedback. John Burnham's (2005) relational reflexivity invites clients into the reflexive process by asking them to reflect on how the conversation is going. We can simply ask unobtrusive questions from time to time during the conversation rather than just at the end, such as: 'How does my style of listening fit for you?' 'Are we going in the right direction?' and so on. This could be described as 'checking out', 'talking about talk', or asking 'questions about questions' (pp. 12–14).

The ethical aspiration of relational reflexivity Burnham says, involves:

The intention, desire, processes, and practice through which therapists and clients explicitly engage one another in coordinating their resources so as to create a relationship with therapeutic potential. (p. 4)

We do this by: 'initiating, responding to, and developing opportunities to consider, explore, experiment with, and elaborate the ways in which . . . [clients] relate' (p. 4).

I began to notice that every time I tried asking a question or making a connection Vince added another explanation or told me yet another story. Maybe he thought that in order for me to understand him I needed to know his 'whole story'? Or maybe he was so pleased to find someone who was willing to listen to him that he wanted to tell me everything about him, 'warts and all'? I wanted to ask how Vince was experiencing our conversation and find some way to check out whether he was finding my listening style useful. But would he allow me to interrupt the flow?

Gregory Bateson (1972) believes that 'warm' ideas are more acceptable than 'cold' ideas, something that John Burnham says we can use to prepare clients for certain kinds of interventions. This is not 'warm' as in 'cuddly' or friendly, since some clients may be suspicious of professionals who are 'too friendly'. We 'warm the context' by 'readying' it, making it more inviting, less scary, by asking 'questions about questions' so that clients don't feel that they have been put on the spot when we explore certain themes and ask certain kinds of questions (pp. 4–8).

I had 'warmed' the context by showing Vince that I was willing to connect with his communication style. Now I asked tentatively, 'Would it be OK with you if I asked you a couple of questions? When Vince replied, 'Sure,' I added, 'You've given me so much wonderful information already. How's it going, talking to me? Is the conversation what you were hoping for?'

'Yeah, it's OK, good', he said, nodding vigorously.

'Good? What's the best bit?'

'You're listening to me,' he said, emphasising the word 'me'. He took a breath and for the first time leaned right back in the chair, his legs stretched out in front of him. He then leaned forward again and launched into the story of being angry with his managers, talking about the unfairness and his fears about losing his job. I decided that the context was 'warm' enough for me to join the conversation more fully. He seemed to enjoy talking to me. But was this enough to make it a therapeutic conversation?

'Would it be OK', I asked, 'to check something out with you?' He nodded. 'You said to Marianne that you wanted help. Is this the kind of thing you had in mind?'

In reply he burst out, 'They offered me anger management, but it was rubbish. I wanted one-to-one.' I felt excited; here was no reluctant client.

Systemic empathy

Carl Rogers (1957) described empathy as necessary and sufficient for positive therapeutic change. In later refinements he says that the therapist does not just reflect the client's feelings back to them, but tests understandings and checks perceptions, clarifying not only the meanings of which the client is aware but 'even those just below the level of awareness' (1986: pp. 135–6).

Since the emergence of briefer, more active therapeutic approaches particularly family therapy, the concept of empathy now includes an understanding of the broader contexts in the client's life, the communication networks, patterns and relationships (Mary Wilkinson 1992: p. 194). Whilst not specifically named in systemic and family approaches, empathy is still at the heart of therapy and is 'the great taken-for-granted of therapy' (Ron Perry 1993: p. 63).

The social constructionist equivalent of empathy is 'coordination' (Mark Chidgey 2002: p. 7). Coordination involves entering a client's 'grammar': by joining their communication style and their language we show empathy. This helps us make connections and understand their 'logic', the meanings they give for their actions (Cronen and Lang 1994). Coordination takes place when we communicate in a way that brings into being people's 'visions of what is necessary, noble, and good . . . and precludes the enactment of what they fear, hate or despise' (Pearce 1989: p. 32). Clients are more likely to feel that we are empathising with them if we address the complexity of their whole life, including all their relevant relationships. Working with these complex patterns of communication is vitally important because, as Gregory Bateson (1979) says, if we locate empathy primarily 'in' only one part of the therapeutic system [the therapist], we are ignoring the processes and complex *patterns of interaction* that take place within every context (pp. 8–9). As we listen we can ask ourselves what other voices are not being heard, why this particular voice is dominant and not some other, what voices are being silenced. Empathising only with certain voices, or facets of a person, can make us overlook 'shy' descriptions about a person that could be hiding behind the dominant ones. Working empathically with the important others in the client's life means that we acknowledge the complexity of their relationships and that everybody is doing the best they can, given all the circumstances. Selective empathy, such as allying with one person against another, can create difficulties of loyalty for the client.

In order to 'coordinate' with Vince and show that I respected his wish to discuss certain themes in a particular way, I connected with his style of talking, which was to re-tell stories in a passionate way using 'strong' language. In order to make an empathic connection with him I occasionally used his language, which we both found entertaining. He showed this by his unwavering eye-contact and frankness and when I checked this out with him he confirmed that I did have an empathic understanding of his world.

I also explored the relationships he had with the key people in the organisation where we both worked.

Now, I invited him to tell me in detail about the recent episode that had brought him to me, including all the relevant people. He described being anxious all weekend because of the new set of responsibilities he'd been given.

When he'd driven onto the campus that Monday morning, he said, after an anxious, sleepless weekend and only just in time for work, he was frustrated by not being able to park because a visiting film crew had taken up all the parking spaces with their trucks. After a short squabble he'd sworn at a crew member. The man, he said, was 'cocky'; he represented everything Vince disliked about privileged people.

So you didn't want to be late for work?' I said, wanting to acknowledge the quieter voices that showed his capabilities and his conscientious approach to work, not just the loud, recriminating ones that said life was unfair and he was in the wrong.

I wanted to explore the relevant people involved. 'I'm wondering . . . when Jack [his manager] brought you to us and asked us to help you, what d'you think he was hoping for?

'He's a good bloke,' Vince replied, 'he wanted to help me'.

'Yes, and he must think something of you to want to help you,' I said.

Vince nodded. 'Yes, I'm a grafter.'

'So he'd agree with me that you're a responsible worker, conscientious?'

Vince liked these different descriptions: 'conscientious' and 'hardworking' rather than 'hot-headed' and 'a problem'.

Now I noticed that we had more of a dialogue. Earlier, when I had tried to interrupt his flow Vince had simply told more stories. 'Is this going OK?' Is it what you had in mind?' I asked.

'Yeah,' he said, enthusiastically. 'It's what I've been asking for, for ages.'

This helped me feel more confident about checking out some other things, to help me understand his 'logic' further.

'When you were on your way here today, what were you feeling . . . um . . . hoping I'd understand about you?' I asked.

I was fearful at first,' he answered. 'I was shaking before I came here.'

This was amazing; while other people had been frightened of him, he'd been afraid of coming to talk to me. 'You don't seem to be shaking now' I said. 'No way,' he replied, and we both burst out laughing.

Another way of thinking about systemic empathy is to think about 'fit'; 'fit' suggests compatibility. The metaphor of the key and the lock is useful here; key and lock don't need to 'match' each other perfectly since many keys shaped differently will have a good enough fit to open the same lock (Ernst von Glaserfeld 1984: pp. 20–1).

The idea that Vince was a 'responsible worker' and 'conscientious' fitted just as well as the idea that he was an 'angry' or 'rude' man and were more appreciative, and more useful, descriptions.

Now I felt able to ask what he hoped for in the future.

'I want to be normal . . . Happy. How I used to be,' he said. The way he relaxed into the chair, his words and his ironic tone gave me hope; he knew what it was like to be a happy person.

Empathic imagination

Albert Einstein (1931) is well known as saying, 'Imagination is more important than knowledge.' He goes on to say, 'For knowledge is limited, whereas imagination embraces the entire world, stimulating progress, giving birth to evolution . . .' (p. 97).

Because of the very real differences between us, I realised that it was important for me to be able to empathically imagine how Vince viewed the world.

The power of imagination is the 'capacity for letting new worlds shape our understandings of ourselves . . . narrative imagination opens us to the foreign world of others by enabling us to tell or hear other stories', according to French philosopher Paul Ricoeur (in Kearney 1996: p. 173).

> Are we not ready to recognize the power of imagination, no longer simply the faculty of deriving 'images' from our sensory experience, but the capacity for letting new worlds shape our understandings of ourselves? Imagination would thus be treated as a dimension of language. In this way, a new link would appear between imagination and metaphor. (Ricoeur 1972: pp. 93–112)

Imagination in 'its multifarious expressions in symbol, metaphor, myth, dream, narrative and . . . social imaginary' is a preoccupation of Paul Ricoeur', Richard Kearney (1996) says (p. 173). Although we are always interpreting, translating 'the foreign into the familiar, the discordant into the concordant, the different into the analogous, the other into the self (or at best, the enlarged "representative self") [and] can never be sure of escaping the hermeneutic circle' (p. 185).

Playing with the Einstein quote, Peter Lang and Elsbeth McAdam say that 'Imagination is knowledge having fun' (McAdam and Lang 2009: p. 110). This, they say, was coined at '10.30 pm after a bottle of wine'. We can have fun using our imagination. But this doesn't mean that the therapist has free rein to imagine bizarre ideas; it can mean being playful or can simply mean acknowledging that another person's experiences are always unique to them and therefore different from ours. Indeed, if we 'notice' too many similarities between us and the client we may have ignored the other person's unique perspectives. Observing the details, the minutiae of the other person's stories helps us explore their worldview and can open up possibilities we had not before considered.

To imaginatively wonder what another person might be experiencing requires the complex ability to take different positions; being steeped in our own cultural and social position we sometimes 'see' and 'hear' certain things and do not notice other things. Empathic imagination requires a broadening of our repertoires of stories so that we are able to find a way to appreciate another person's different 'logic' and different ways of describing the world. As John Keats (1947) says of Shakespeare, he possesses a 'Negative Capability', an ability to 'wonder', to 'wait in uncertainties', to 'imagine into the life of the other . . . capable of being in uncertainties, mysteries, doubts, without any irritable reaching after fact or reason' (p. 72).

Vince and I were different in numerous ways including gender, life experiences and our professional life. When he talked in a disparaging way about his ex-wives it was initially hard to be empathic with him, especially when he was cheekily flirtatious with me. But, rather than showing that I was affronted by his views, I tried to make an imaginative connection with him, to imagine what life could be like from his position. In order to coordinate with his worldview and develop empathy with him I had to make an imaginative leap, make a temporary shift from my own position.

I reflected on the unfairness of the long-term effects of the head injury and I decided that this could be a good time to ask about how he'd sustained it. When I asked him he told me that he'd risked his own life to rescue some students from a fire in a building on the campus, even though he had not been on duty. Nobody had appreciated how Vince's quick thinking had saved lives and he was now living with the after-effects, which were making him forgetful and irritable. I wondered what this must be like.

He went on to tell me about another time when he was on duty and had chased after intruders, boys on motorbikes, who seemed to be trying to break in to the university. He said he'd warned his managers but nobody had taken any notice and instead of being thanked he'd been reprimanded for chasing them. Then, a few days later, computer equipment was stolen. Nobody acknowledged that this could have been prevented if they'd listened to Vince.

I wondered what it might be like to be an 'action man'; I was curious about how he'd responded to the fire. 'Let me see if I've got this right, the fire, you saved their lives?'

'I did . . . but because of that I got the head injury. And since then I keep losing my temper over every little thing – it's the head injury. They don't realise . . .' He would have continued in this vein, but now I felt more able to interrupt, to explore some different aspects of the story.

If we are to help someone bring about any changes some of the most important things we can say to them are 'Stop! Look! Listen!' says John Shotter (2005), drawing on Wittgenstein (1953): 'we can break into the routine flow of their activity; we can "deconstruct" their practice in practice; and in so doing bring their attention to aspects of their own activity previously unnoticed by them'.

'Were the students grateful?'

'Yes, every time I see them they thank me,' Vince answered.

'It sounds like you were a bit of a hero – helping those people escape the fire, risking your own life?'

'The fire brigade told me I shouldn't have done it, but if I hadn't . . . who knows . . . maybe . . . I dread to think what would have happened to them. And I wasn't even on duty . . .'

'So, would you say you're a person who cares about people, wants to help people?'

'I do. I'll do anything to help anyone, never mind who they are.'

'You rushed in to help those people, not even thinking about your own safety?'

'That's when I got the head injury. I've had dreadful headaches since then as well as the temper. And those boys on motorbikes . . . No-one's ever thanked me. All they ever do is tell you that you've done something wrong.'

'So, you're what the papers might call a "have-a-go hero"?'

Vince smiled. He looked thoughtful. 'Yes, you could say so . . . All they did was tell me off. I got a warning . . . and they're taking it into account now, because of this latest business. I might get suspended.'

I heard this but decided instead to explore the new story to see if it fitted. 'It's kind of like you were a, you know, a knight on a white charger. D'you know what I mean?'

'Yes – I'm a nice bloke. A Kind Vince. I'm not a Nasty Vince . . .'

We laughed. Although these were new descriptions, I reflected that there was a strong theme of 'unfairness' running through Vince's stories. I recalled the family story he'd told me earlier: he had been terrorised by his 'father' throughout his childhood. As a child Vince didn't know that he'd been the result of a wartime romance between his mother and her husband's brother, and he'd only found out later in life. His 'father' had treated him differently from the other children (who were his biological children) and had beaten him regularly until the day Vince was old enough to stand up for himself and Vince had beaten him up. After that he became known as someone who was ready to fight, being particularly keen to defend an injustice and stand up for 'the underdog'.

I reflected that a man whose identity had been forged out of an accident of birth and had been punished severely because of it may have had a sense of the unfairness of life, wanting to seek justice. But I wanted to check this out.

'When you were a kid, the man you called your dad gave you a hard time . . . perhaps you wished someone had stood up for you . . . ? You had it rough . . . I'm wondering . . . you're the kind of person who stands up for people, wants to help people . . . ?'

'Yeah, I'll help anyone . . . it wasn't right, those boys rode in . . . then they came back and stole all that stuff . . .'

'Rushing in to protect the university's property, saving those students – now worrying all weekend because of all the extra responsibility and finding you couldn't park?'

'And all they want to do is put me on a warning . . . I might get suspended . . . might even lose my job . . . But I'll help anybody, me . . . I want to help people . . .'

'Do they realise how you take your job seriously, how hard-working you are, loyal and conscientious?' I said.

'That's right. I'm not a bad person. I might be a bit rough, but I'm a gentle giant, me, always trying to help someone.'

Making these connections with Vince's 'logic' helped me to imagine in an empathic way what it could feel like to be him, to appreciate things from his position. I began to feel differently about him. Rather than describing him as an 'aggressive' man from a tough background, a flirtatious, philandering 'sexist' man, he was a person who had stood up for himself after a miserable childhood; he was, in his own description, a 'softie' who cared deeply for others, an advocate for justice and a conscientious worker.

As we came to the end of that conversation Vince told me that he had a relationship with June, but that it had 'no future'. I heard the negativity in his voice and said I could see them together if this would be helpful. He eagerly accepted.

June was keen to come with Vince. And I asked my colleague Heleni Andreadi to join me. We had eight couple sessions with them at fortnightly or monthly intervals. June always saw her position as coming to help Vince but we inevitably, perhaps surreptitiously, worked on their relationship as a whole, and explored their relationship and many misunderstandings in lively conversations. Vince and June confronted their differences, including Vince's jealousy of June's friendship with her ex-mother-in-law. And he began to question his life-long 'chauvinistic' views about women.

Vince and June often told us that they found the couple sessions useful.

Heleni and I 'pointed out' Vince's and June's abilities and resources, and they noticed each other's skills and abilities. We used self–other-reflexivity and systemic empathy to develop our ability to empathically imagine life from their different positions.

The meetings came to a natural conclusion: Vince was less volatile; he and June developed a stronger relationship; he was back at work, the suspension lifted, helped by a report which Vince and I wrote together. He said he was a 'different' man, rarely irritable and able to take set-backs and frustrations in his stride.

Review/Research

After we had finished working together I bumped into Vince and asked if he and June would be willing to review the therapy. He gladly agreed and came on his own. June wanted to come but had work commitments.

'What do you remember about being brought into the Centre?' I asked. 'You seemed pretty angry at the time.'

'Angry?' he laughed. 'That's an understatement. I was in cuckoo-land – on another plane – in another time.'

'When you got that phone call from me, what did you think?'

'I thought, "thank God somebody's listening at last".'

'And that first meeting . . . ?'

'I was fearful at first – I was shaking beforehand. But at the end I was delighted – I wanted to come back, the next day . . . every day,' he laughed. We all laughed.

'How was that?' I asked.

'You listened to me. You gave me 100% of you. You were concerned about me. I thought, "Someone's interested – at last!" I'd been asking for help for a long time – I had anger management in a group but there were too many people. I wanted one-to-one. I felt secure, and when you said bring June, I thought "that's it; that does it for me – I'll have some of that". . .'

'And the couple sessions with June . . . how did they help?' Heleni asked.

'She enjoys coming here – she didn't want me coming without her.'

'What helped her, do you think?'

'She liked seeing me listening to other people – she saw me listening to you two. I listen to what you say.'

After some more talking Heleni said, 'I was thinking about your humour . . .'

'You liked my jokes – you understand what I'm saying,' Vince replied. 'I felt comfortable because you understood my humour. I can cry if I want to, I can be as I am with you two. I felt comfortable with you. I'm happy again. I'm laughing again.

'You learned me [taught me] when I should open and shut my mouth. You were straight with me from the beginning. I wanted that. That's what I needed. You could advise me the best thing – you told me "let everything go" – when I'm in my car now I don't get angry – I let it all go. I'm a Gentle Giant. I wouldn't hurt anybody . . . You saw that, they didn't.'

Referring to an assessment he'd had recently with a psychologist Vince said, 'She didn't seem interested in me. She seemed half asleep. She was miserable and strait-laced.'

It was fortunate that my style and Heleni's fitted with Vince and June.

At the end of the conversation Vince said, 'You've done it. Without your help I wouldn't be here today. I can't take defeat. I'm too proud – I broke and you got me back out of it.'

Postcript

Several months later Vince rang to ask if he could come to see me; he sounded angry and upset and said June was 'infuriating' and 'getting on his nerves'. I was concerned by his agitated tone. But he didn't turn up for the appointment.

Then in a surprise twist, a month or so later, Vince asked for an urgent appointment. He arrived looking uncomfortable and 'confessed' that he'd been having an affair with another woman for a long time. He said he felt ashamed of the way he'd treated both women, neither of whom deserved it. We talked through the options. I had often been forthright with Vince and this fitted for him and he said he valued this. But I didn't comment on Vince's life-long tendency to two-time his partners: he knew that I knew. I didn't approve of him two-timing June, but there was no need to say so because of the self-reflexivity he'd developed.

An ability to use systemic empathy and empathic imagination with a client whose behaviour offends our moral code can be challenging; therapy involves the ability to make sense of a person's actions, to take a generous and imaginative leap from our own position whilst not betraying our own ethical stance.

I bumped into Vince some weeks later. He said that he'd ended the affair and had 'settled down happily' with June. Again he thanked me profusely. This, I felt, was a good ending to the work.

The conversations Heleni and I had had with Vince and June had helped him develop some new, respectful self-descriptions, which helped him believe in the possibility of having an honest relationship with June. By helping both of them notice their competencies and by using humour Heleni and I were able to challenge some of Vince's less-than-helpful stories about women, which helped him develop more appreciative ways of behaving towards June. And for the first time in his life, he decided to make a commitment to one woman.

Reflexive questions:

When you are talking with a client:

- What are you communicating?
- What is this inviting?
- How is the client responding to your invitations?
- How would you know if the client is finding the conversation useful, or not?
- What personal resources are you drawing on?
- How do you show empathy towards the client and the important people in their life?
- How do you show empathic imagination?

Reflect on a time when you were able to leave your own 'safe position' to enter the client's world:

- How were you able to do this?
- What effect did this have on them and your therapeutic work?

8

FURTHER IDEAS AND RESOURCES FOR SUPERVISORS

Supervision is a multifaceted activity and supervisors are at the intersection of at least three systems: (a) the client's, (b) the therapist's, and (c) the supervisor's, each of which has its own language and 'rules'. The organisational contexts, including those in which the supervisor and therapist work as well as the therapist's work or training context, also play their part.

Supervisors can use reflexivity to pay attention to the way 'reality' is co-constructed in these relationships. Johnella Bird (2006) writes supervision as super-vision 'in order to imply a process which enhances vision' (p. 112). And she says that 'one of the principal tasks of super-vision is to liberate the mind in order to foster the counsellor's sense of creativity' (p. 4).

In this chapter I discuss:

(a) 'parallel' processes;
(b) 'first order' and 'second order' positions;
(c) 'mapping' personal and professional stories;
(d) 'prismatic dialogue'.

As it is impossible for an 'observer' to describe any situation without including oneself, it is important that supervisors acknowledge the ways we are always 'self-referencing', making connections with what we already know (Elkaim 1990: pp. 54–71). Another interrelated concept is 'resonance'; therapists and supervisors notice the stories that 'resonate' for us, not in a way that searches for the 'truth', but as a way of making a 'unique bridge' or connection between us and others (p. 97).

Reflexivity can help supervisors explore how meanings are co-constructed in the 'couplings' at these 'intersection points', helping us work with the inherent contradictions and competing demands between all these contexts so we can move creatively between many different positions.

In supervision the first priority is towards the client, ensuring that clients receive the highest possible quality of service. The second responsibility is towards the supervisee, so 'that they experience an enabling, facilitative, safe, learning, and developmental practice opportunity from the supervisor', and the third responsibility is to the team, or group of supervisees (Vivienne Gross 2002: pp. 126–7).

In this chapter I discuss a one-to-one supervisory conversation with Tessa, a trainee therapist. We had been meeting for some months and had developed a good working relationship when she told me about Tom, a young client who made her feel so frustrated and angry that she felt like hitting him. I felt alarmed at hearing this and used my reactions to explore stories from Tom's position, Tessa's and my own.

It is useful to clarify the difference between supervision and consultation:

(a) Supervision: a supervisor is a trainer or manager of the supervisee and there is a hierarchical relationship.
(b) Consultation: the supervisor has no statutory or clinical responsibility for the work of the person who consults them. (Elsa Jones 2003: p. 7)

I was Tessa's supervisor, as she was still in training, and I had accepted clinical responsibility for the work she did in both contexts in which she worked.

Laura Fruggeri (2002) describes two kinds of supervision:

(i) teaching a specific psychotherapeutic approach: the focus is the therapist's learning process, what they do, could do, how they think and so on;
(ii) helping the therapist reflect on their practice: the focus is on the level of co-construction and 'interdependence', between therapist and client (p. 20).

One could add a third:

(iii) reflection for both supervisor and therapist: the focus is on what they are co-constructing in their relationship.

Supervisors often use all three approaches.

Forms of supervision

There are advantages and drawbacks to every form of supervision. 'Live' supervision, where the supervisor works from behind a one-way screen or via a monitor, sometimes with a therapy team, is the preferred method in systemic family therapy. Live supervision can be tremendously energising for all, and can enhance therapists' opportunities for self-reflexivity. At its best, the client benefits from on-the-spot ideas from the supervisor, who is able to take a different position from that of the therapist. Supervisors can notice the rich patterns of interactions between the therapist and the client as they emerge.

In this model the 'five-part-session', created by the Milan group (Selvini Palazzoli et al. 1980), offers at least three opportunities for reflexive conversations:

(a) pre-session reflection – before the meeting;
(b) inter-session reflection – co-creating ideas in a break during the conversation;
(c) post-session reflection – reflecting after the meeting, on the patterns that have been co-created.

Therapists working with a colleague or a team therapist can have a 'reflecting team' (Tom Andersen 1987; 1990) and explore multiple perspectives in front of the client(s), which the client can respond to and comment on. This more egalitarian approach enables clients to hear many voices and become involved in reflexive conversations with the therapists.

The advantage of 'indirect' or 'reported' supervision is that it gives therapists opportunities to explore their presuppositions and style of working before and after therapy; the supervisor and therapist can explore the patterns between therapist and client in a less pressured environment. The therapist can make connections between theory and practice away from the therapy, giving time for 'reflection-on-action' (Schon 1987).

In reported supervision, therapists can bring video and audio tapes and transcripts that show the patterns of interaction in their conversations with clients. A video tape provides opportunities for therapists to notice the 'non-verbal dances' as well as the verbal content; an audio tape allows supervisor and therapist to hear the tone and pace of each voice, whilst a transcript helps therapist and supervisor reflect on a small piece of interaction.

In the piece of work I discuss below, Tessa brought a short transcript and audio tape. She told me that after four meetings with Tom he was feeling just as miserable about himself as when he had first come to talk to her. I became curious about what stories and patterns were being co-created in their conversations and wondered how this was affecting her stories about her abilities and about Tom and his networks of relationships.

About eighteen months before this conversation I had been asked by a small university to find a trainee to provide therapy for their students. When Tessa, a Black British woman in her late 20s doing a Master's in Psychological Counselling, came for an interview for a placement with me I was so impressed with her curiosity, intelligence and enthusiasm that I recommended her for this position. She began to work there one day a week as well as seeing clients at my service on another day.

Fortunately we were a good 'fit': I appreciated her sparky style and eagerness to learn and she gradually began to trust me. The conversation I discuss here stands out for me as one in which I risked exploring some of her personal and professional stories that seemed to be influencing her therapeutic work. It demonstrates the way that supervisors have to manage the intersection between many 'systems'.

Creating a contract for supervision is crucial (Michael Carroll 1996: pp. 97–9).

From the outset I created a clear contract with Tessa, clarifying expectations, outlining practicalities, issues of accountability and forms of assessment, which we reviewed from time to time. At the beginning of every meeting I checked with her what she wanted to focus on and how I could be helpful to her. And at various points I invited her to let me know how our conversation was going and how my theoretical ideas fitted with hers.

Because of her openness to learn and her willingness to let me know what was useful and what she found less useful I began to introduce more creative and reflexive ways of working and became more open with her. When our work came to an end I asked her for feedback on the supervision and she said that being 'allowed' to use humour in conversations with me made her 'feel safe and able to take risks'. 'It made it easier to hear what you were saying. I could take a different position and try new things with my clients. Before, I was afraid that humour would be seen as unprofessional.'

Not all supervisors and therapists are comfortable with using humour but I find it helps me reframe, reformulate and make creative leaps, which creates a context in which we can address difficult issues, if necessary.

In supervision I used:

■ direct 'teaching' input;
■ 'relational reflexivity';
■ self-disclosure;
■ 'mapping';
■ 'prismatic dialogue'.

These practices helped us notice the 'patterns' that were being co-created between:

■ *Tessa and Tom;*
■ *Tom and the important people in his life;*
■ *Tessa and me.*

We co-construct the 'dance'

As Heinz von Foerster (1984) notes, the 'observer' always becomes part of any system; when we meet a client we become part of their 'system'. We are not independent of what we are observing; the 'observer' always describes the world by making distinctions, but these descriptions are self-referential or reflexive; a 'description, when carefully inspected, reveals the properties of the observer' (Francisco Varela 1975: p. 22, in Elkaim 1990: p. 63). However, Varela (1988) warns that when we talk of 'including' the observer we run the risk of suggesting that there is an entity called 'the observer' independent of what is being observed, whereas we can never be separate from any 'system' or context we enter. Indeed, each of us emerges in the act of 'observation' through how we describe clients and supervisees, what we say and do in conversations with them.

What we notice, what 'resonates' for us, reveals aspects of ourselves; we cannot speak of a client, a couple or a family and their worldviews without speaking at the same time of the worldviews of the therapist and the supervisor. 'Everything that the therapist is telling us is the result of a structural coupling,' Mony Elkaim (1990: p. 100) says, drawing on Humberto Maturana (1983). 'Structural coupling' refers to the way humans and animals all have possibilities and limitations: a fish can swim easily but can't run up a tree like a cat. To extend this metaphor we look for what appears to 'fit' in the way a person describes and acts in the world, which can seem to be the only possible way of being in the world, at that point in time (Peter Lang and Elsbeth McAdam 1995: p. 82). Reflexive therapists are fascinated by the kinds of stories that 'fit' for us, what we notice and don't notice.

I recall a conversation I had with Jody, another supervisee: Jody and I were excited because Petra, who Jody had been seeing for some months, was going to bring her mother for the first time. Jody and I were going to work together and we were co-creating ideas and exploring possible hypotheses in a pre-session conversation. After some time I noticed that we were discussing Petra's relationships with her mother and her sister but not her relationship with her father. As soon as I noticed this we looked at the genogram; the father was clearly there and living in the family but, for some reason, we had ignored him.

I told Jody that I might have inadvertently forgotten about Petra's father because I had grown up in a home without a father. Jody said that she, too, had grown up without a father. We were fascinated and wondered if our own personal stories had encouraged us to 'see' the daughter–mother relationship but not the daughter–father relationship.

The ideas discussed above come from approaches known as 'constructivism': the meanings we give for events in the world arise from our individual experiences; people make sense of their world through sets of premises and beliefs. The constructivist focus on the individual was criticised by social constructionist thinkers, who widened this to take into account the way people co-construct meaning through communication processes and the language we use (Kenneth Gergen 1999; 2001; Rom Harré 1995; Rom Harré and Grant Gillett 2005; Barnett Pearce 1994; 2007; John Shotter 1993; 2005).

Although these two positions are considered 'oppositional', Laura Fruggeri (2002) views them as being 'intertwined' and recommends a both/and approach. It is more useful, she says, to notice that 'the level of co-construction and the level of individual construction are linked through a recursive process' (pp. 4–6):

> while the participants in the interaction are engaged in these complex symbolic, behavioural, strategic, and self-validating processes, they also initiate a 'dance' . . . [a] coordination of behaviours, joint action, language game – through which they negotiate and co-construct meanings, identities, relationships, roles, and social realities . . . what people do together. (pp. 5–6)

When Petra and her mother came for the meeting I metaphorically brought Petra's father's voice into the conversation right away and was amazed to hear how concerned he was about his daughter. Petra was surprised and this new information enriched the conversation.

Returning now to the supervision conversation with Tessa, which for practical purposes was 'reported', not live supervision, first I asked how I could be useful to her. Tessa said she had seen her client Tom every week for four weeks and was seeing no improvement. She wanted to know how to help him feel better.

She'd made an audio tape of their last conversation and had written a short transcript, which we worked on. I asked her how she wanted me to respond; she wanted to describe Tom, who, she said, was a twenty-year-old student. He was lonely, had financial difficulties and was unable to get a part-time job. He desperately wanted to be able to date girls but felt too shy to make the first move. Tom had come to Britain from America to study; he described his relationship with his parents as 'not good', although he had followed his mother's suggestion to have counselling.

'How does Tom respond to you?' I asked Tessa.

'He likes coming,' Tessa said. 'He's always on time and says he likes talking to me.'

'Great.'

'But,' Tessa continued, 'he's always so pessimistic. And nothing changes. He turns up the next time feeling even more miserable.'

'So, how does that affect you?'

'I feel, I don't know, I get so angry with myself.'

'Angry?'

'Yeah, because nothing's changing.'

Tom's stories of 'hopelessness' arose within his peer group, where other students seemed to have more money and a better social life than he did.

Parallel process

There are many explanations of 'parallel process', most from psychoanalytic and psychodynamic literature, where it is seen as a form of transference (Carroll 1996: pp. 103–8). Also known as 'reflexive' or 'reflection process', 'mirroring' and 'parallel re-enactment', this refers to feelings and themes that appear to be similar in the relationship between supervisor and therapist and therapist and client. Michael Carroll warns that this 'fascinating and little understood phenomenon of . . . supervision . . . can too easily become a magical formula for clever interpretation and woolly connections . . . and can be utterly incomprehensible and threatening to supervisees, especially beginners' (p. 103). However, 'Systems theory and systemic approaches could well contribute to our understanding of parallel process' (pp. 106–7).

The idea that similar stories can be co-created within both the supervisor /therapist system and the client/therapist system because of communication processes is described by Bernard and Goodyear (1992) as 'isomorphism'. This does move away from viewing these processes as intrapsychic but, Italian systemic therapist Laura Fruggeri (Peter Lang 2006) says, 'there is no isomorphism between the client's world and our world. . . . What is known as the "parallel process" ignores huge differences in power and so on between people who are in different positions.'

'What enters into play in supervision . . . is an intersection between elements tied to the therapist and to the . . . [client], but also to the supervisor, to the rules of the institution where the therapy takes place, to the rules of the supervision group, etc.' And, 'what we call transference and countertransference is only the tip of a much larger iceberg . . .' (Elkaim 1990: p. 88).

Tom was feeling despondent, as was Tessa. Tessa also felt angry with the unchanging nature of the therapy. Tom, it later turned out, also felt 'angry'. However, I did not feel despondent, angry or frustrated towards Tessa or Tom. I preferred to be curious about the way these feelings had been co-constructed within specific conversations. I wanted to respect Tessa's view of Tom and at the same time 'open space' for her to develop some different stories and take a different position towards him.

Tessa sometimes felt frustrated with the referral system in the institution where she saw Tom, as well as with the demands of her training course. Could these perhaps be influencing her conversations with Tom, and our relationship?

'First order' and 'second order' positions in supervision

In the early 1980s there was a paradigm shift in family therapy approaches from taking 'first order' positions to taking 'second order' positions (Hoffman 1985). The terms 'first order' and 'second order' are contractions of 'first order/second order cybernetics', referring to the idea that 'feedback loops' (cybernetics) are important in communication processes (Bateson 1972). A therapist taking a first order position focuses on the client, on just one part of the 'system', such as saying, 'Why does the client feel so hopeless?'

In moving to a second order perspective there is more emphasis on noticing the interpersonal patterns (Bateson 1972; 1979) that are being co-created by everything that is taking place within the client's relationships, between the therapist and the client and between the supervisor and therapist. However, despite accepting that 'second order' approaches are considered invaluable, there tends to be 'a magnet-like attraction' for discussing client-focused issues rather than looking at the practitioner's developing abilities (Gross 2002: p. 119).

A supervisor who takes a 'second order' position is curious about the patterns we are co-creating with the therapist about their relationship with the client, as well as the client's networks of relationships. All these communication processes are mutually influential. As Mony Elkaim (1990) says, 'It is far richer to think about the function and meaning of the feeling experienced in relation to the whole system than to limit one's hypotheses to purely internal dynamics' (p. 111).

I wanted to be curious about:

- *Tessa's relationship with Tom;*
- *Tom's relationship with the important people in his life;*
- *my relationship with Tessa;*
- *the 'rules' of Tessa's training course;*
- *the rules of the organisation where she saw Tom;*
- *the rules of my organisational/work context;*
- *our professional Code of Ethics;*
- *our own personal and professional stories.*

As noted, supervisors are not detached observers; we are involved in co-constructing stories about our own identity, the therapist's identity and the client's (including the client's relationships with people in their life).

Transcript: developing reflexivity

In the first few minutes of the first session, there are an enormous number of interactions between the client(s) and the therapist. And what seem to be 'trivial elements often determine the entire course of the session' (Elkaim 1990). For example, 'if you start with the idea that the mother is emotional, you may create a system where she is in fact emotional' (p. 109).

It is difficult not to participate in creating the thing we think we see. . . . What is felt in itself is unique, but it is amplified and maintained by its context; what the protagonists in a therapeutic system experience is both linked to themselves and not reducible to them.   (p. 111)

Using the transcript Tessa had written from the audio tape, we read aloud, with Tessa speaking her own words whilst I read Tom's words, using his pace and tone, as she described. We didn't listen to the audio tape because of time constraints.

Tom had arrived for his fourth conversation with Tessa feeling miserable and angry, because a few days before, on Valentine's Day, he had received a parcel of books from his parents.

Tom's is the first voice. He is referring to the parcel.

'Yeah, and when I opened it, there were all these stupid self-help books, like "Dating" and like, "How to Chat up Girls" – all that stuff. Can you believe they did that?'

Tessa (reading her own words): 'Was it your mum or dad who sent them?'

Me (as Tom): 'My mum probably; that's the sort of thing she'd do.'

'Did she put a note in with them?' *Tessa asked.*

'Yeah, a card.'

'A card?'

'Yeah, a card with a heart; a Valentine card! Like, I'd want something like that from my mum?'

'Did she write a message?'

'Yeah, something sloppy. And she said something like, "Hope these help you . . .".'

'Hmmm,' *Tessa said,* 'I wonder if you felt humiliated?'

Me (as Tom): silence 'Yeah . . .'

Hearing Tessa use the word 'humiliated' gave me a frisson of alarm; I noticed Tom's hesitation and was curious about how it might have affected him and his relationship with his mother.

We stopped reading from the transcript. 'How did the conversation go after that?' *I asked Tessa.*

'He got more and more negative,' Tessa replied.

'If Tom were here now, how would he say he felt at the end of that conversation?'

'He'd say he was miserable, even more fed up.'

'I'm wondering. Tessa,' I said, 'what gave you the idea to use the word "humiliated"?'

'It was everything he'd said about his parents, hating them and feeling that they didn't understand him. And then getting the parcel . . . I felt so sorry for him; that's what I thought he must be feeling . . .'

'How were you hoping he'd respond?' I asked her.

'I hoped he'd feel understood – that I'd heard him.'

'Where did you get the idea to use that word?'

Supervisors have a responsibility to ask a therapist to explain their theoretical knowledge and the theories that would support or contradict what they did.   (Peter Lang 2009)

She said that a tutor had told the students that it was important to 'be authentic' and 'congruent' when responding to clients so they felt you had really understood them.

We are obligated to use different styles in supervision. In the same way that therapists can 'introduce some difference' by playing with different styles, so can supervisors. Working in a collaborative way does not mean being mild or gentle all the time; we could ask, 'You said what? Didn't that make you shudder?'   (Lang 2009).

Tessa said that another supervisor had reprimanded her for being 'too much in her head', saying, 'don't think from the head; feel from the gut'.

'I felt it in my gut, that he would be feeling humiliated,' she said now.

'What did you feel in your gut?'

'I imagined what it would be like to receive a parcel like that from your parents and the feeling that came to me was he would feel humiliated.'

'Had he mentioned that feeling before?'

'No,' Tessa said, 'it came from me.'

My dilemma was that I wanted to give priority to Tom and the people who were important to him, in this case his parents; yet I also wanted to explore Tessa's theoretical and professional understandings and help her develop her abilities, so she could be more useful to Tom and other clients.

'The idea that it is important to get one's feelings "out" and that people repress their "real" feelings, which they must bring "out", is a judgement based on individualistic thinking' (Lang 2008). As Vernon Cronen (2007) says, the notion of the 'authentic self' in the language of psychotherapy comes from John Locke's concept that we can distinguish between inner and outer worlds. 'If people say, "I must be true to my true self" this is an idea that identity is fixed, a way of talking that dominated western discourse until we became relational.'

Although I was still curious about how she had decided to use the word 'humiliated', I decided that the ideas I was introducing were challenging enough. Also, I recalled her telling me about a distressing experience when a previous supervisor's response had knocked her fragile confidence. The supervisor had made a formal complaint about her to the tutor on her training course without first discussing it with Tessa. She believed that Tessa had not paid enough attention to a client's grief processes and had followed the client's wish to move on with his life. I admired the way Tessa had handled the formal appeal, which found in her favour.

I decided that it might be more useful to acknowledge her abilities. 'What do you think enabled Tom to be so open with you about his reaction to the parcel?' I asked.

'I guess he was beginning to trust me,' Tessa said. I nodded encouragingly.

Direct teaching

'So, how can I be helpful to you right now?' I asked.

'I want to help Tom next time I see him; can you give me some ideas?'

I saw this as an invitation. 'The language we use co-creates reality,' I said, then asked, 'Would you be interested to hear more?' Tessa said she would love to. I was extremely fortunate to have a supervisee who was so keen to learn.

'Uninvited teaching does not make learning,' says John Holt (1989), 'but – and this was even harder for me to learn – for the most part such teaching prevents learning' (p. 128, in Burnham 1993: p. 358).

I went on to talk about language being 'constitutive', that the words we use create reality and this is why it is useful to be cautious about what we say, the metaphors and ideas that we introduce, even to consider what we choose to 'reflect back' to clients since this language could have long-reaching effects.

'But how can I actually use these ideas?' she asked. 'I want to help him, but I'm obviously not.'

Perhaps this kind of teaching was not practical enough for her?

'If you were helping him, what would you notice?' I asked.

'He'd be feeling better.'

'And you?'

'I'd feel better. I don't think I'm progressing right now.' There was real despair in her voice.

The impact of culture

Tessa was a black British woman. And she was the first person in her family to do a post-graduate degree and professional training; there was no-one in her family to help her with her academic work. We talked briefly about our different stories of culture, colour and class, since neither of us came from the dominant British culture. I empathised with her stories of wanting to 'get it right'.

'I have internal battles about "do I fit in?"' she told me. 'And I'm always beating myself up. In the Caribbean culture we feel we've got to do things better than white people.'

John Burnham and Queenie Harris (2002) write in a humorous way about their 23-year professional relationship and their different cultural, ethnic, class, colour, professional and gender positions. John Burnham is a white family therapist from a working-class background and Queenie Harris is an Indian psychiatrist from a high caste background. They urge practitioners to be 'willing to be "clumsy rather than clever"' when talking about cultural differences, which can make 'initial steps towards "cultural competence" easier to make' (p. 25).

Tessa and I noted that in her family she was seen as 'successful': she was doing a highly demanding professional training at post-graduate level before her thirtieth birthday; this seemed to me to be a young age. Making these connections helped her take a kinder position towards her less confident self. She liked the idea that she was a pioneer in her family and realised she was actually doing extremely well.

'Mapping' personal and professional stories

A component called 'Mapping' used in one systemic therapy training centre in London refers to the way trainee therapists are offered opportunities to explore the way their personal and professional stories affect their therapeutic work (Fran Hedges and Susan Lang 1993: pp. 277–98). At KCC, a systemic training centre in London, a tutor, working with small groups of trainee therapists, encourages them to explore how their stories are affecting their therapeutic work and vice versa.

In family therapy training it has long been accepted that it is helpful for therapists to explore their own family patterns (Murray Bowen 1978).

Connecting to what Tessa had just said, I asked, 'If you were progressing, what do you think you would be doing?'

'I'd feel a sense of confidence.'

'All the time? In every situation?' I wanted her to tell me about the contexts in which these patterns of communication emerged.

'No, but more than I do now, which is never! Nothing I say to Tom makes any difference,' she burst out. 'I get so angry I want to hit him.'

I felt a sense of alarm: my throat constricted, my body felt tense and I wondered what was making her react so strongly. 'Would it be OK, if I asked you something?'

'Sure, anything.'

'I'm wondering if you're making a connection with a personal story?'

In her fascinating book *You Can Go Home Again*, Monica McGoldrick (1995) urges people to explore patterns and 'blind spots' in their families. 'Every facet of your family's biography is part of the many-layered pattern that becomes your identity.' For example, an aunt's suicide leaves 'a legacy of pain, anger, guilt, and social stigma', affecting close family, extended family and future generations (p. 30). Using well-known families she shows how events in a family can affect inter-generational patterns. It is noteworthy, she says, that 'Sigmund Freud . . . focused almost exclusively on the importance of childhood fantasies about parents, ignoring the realities of parents' lives, the role of siblings, and the importance of the extended family.' And little attention has been paid to his mother, who lived to the age of ninety-five. He 'did his best to be sure that his family history would be told the way he intended [and] destroyed many personal and family records' (pp. 23–4).

'I think you're right,' Tessa said thoughtfully. 'I remember my younger sister was depressed for a while. She's not a "doing" person . . . she thinks all the time. If I feel down I just get up and do something. She was just hanging about doing nothing. I tried to help her, but nothing I did made any difference.'

When Tessa was sixteen her mother had become ill and Tessa had taken on the role of carer in her family. She had developed the identity of 'helper', then had taken low status 'caring profession' jobs. Being keen to help people change, fuelled her desire to become a qualified therapist. These stories of wanting to help people to make a difference enabled me to understand her frustration with Tom. Perhaps she was thinking, 'if I couldn't help my sister and I can't help Tom, can I ever be a successful therapist?'

Also, there was an expectation on her course that she should understand and practise at least three different theoretical approaches, which she sometimes found confusing. She said, 'As a trainee, you're serving so many masters. It's frustrating because you don't know what to do.' And I was introducing her to yet another model! This was another context that was influencing her conversations with Tom.

Our identities are continuously being co-created in the communication we have with others, Paul Ricoeur says (in Kearney 1996). As well as developing their therapeutic abilities, therapists in training are developing their identity as a professional. We co-create our professional identities, within our conversations. In this way, 'We not only create communities, relationships, institutions and cultures we also create our identities – our selfhood' (Peter Lang et al. 1990: p. 41).

The professional self cannot be separated from the personal self. . . . In practice a person's many life experiences and ideas may inform their action in different ways at different times . . . the moral position of training is that trainees should become more self-reflexive about the positions they occupy in conversations.   (Hedges and Lang 1993: p. 278)

Tessa was struggling with her professional identity but her willingness to explore the connections between her practice and her personal and family stories made me feel optimistic for her future career as a therapist.

Reflection on patterns and processes

Now I reflected on the 'upbeat', active style and tone of voice I'd heard in her audio tapes with clients, particularly Tom. And I wondered whether this connected with her personal and/or family stories.

'So you're more of a doer . . . ?' I asked.

'Also my cousin was depressed and I couldn't help her either. Nothing I said made any difference,' she added.

'So you want to make a difference, to help people?'

'Yes. And it makes me so . . . mad if I can't help.'

I now realised that there seemed to be a pattern in her conversations with Tom: he would give examples of why his life was miserable and Tessa would show optimism in an 'encouraging' tone of voice and make suggestions. No wonder she would leave these conversations feeling exhausted.

'When I listened to the last tape of you working with Tom,' I said, 'I heard you working incredibly hard, wanting to help and being so caring, as you were in your family.'

'It makes me realise why I've been getting so angry with Tom,' she said.

The aim of supervision, Laura Fruggeri (2002) notes, 'is to move from stories about clients to stories about the relationship between clients and therapists'. This 'second order' position involves focusing on the patterns of interactions between therapist and client, what they *do* together.

Supervisors can help supervisees reflect on the 'interdependence' between them and their clients. This level, she says, stresses the 'dance' between therapist and client, how they coordinate to generate a social reality.

I have adapted her 4-part process:

(1) The therapist tells the story of the therapy.
(2) Supervisor and therapists create a genogram which includes people involved in the client's significant systems, including the therapist and professionals from different agencies.

The supervisor asks how everybody in the family or system understands the situation and how they feel in relation to one another. 'This helps the supervisee to decentralise, to move from, "What am I doing?", "What could I do?" to the more self-reflexive position of, "How does the client see me?", "What does the client think we are doing together?"'

(3) Supervisor and therapist describe what therapist and client do together: do they construct blame on someone, or dependence, or exclusion of others, or autonomy, or space for others?
(4) They reflect how any change would affect other relationships in the client's life.

Therapists recognise how clients are active in therapeutic interventions, that therapy is a joint action, a co-authored script. Gregory Bateson (1972; 1979) has shown us that we can't take total responsibility for what happens in a relationship nor can we refuse to take any responsibility: everybody's actions are mutually influential although some have more power.

Prismatic dialogue

I was thinking about how to explore Tessa's stories about Tom's relationship towards his mother and had an idea about how to do this. 'So, now I'm wondering, how about trying something different?' I asked.

Johnella Bird (2006) developed 'prismatic dialogue' with David Epston in teaching contexts when doing 'super-vision' (p. 2). She uses prismatic dialogue when she thinks the therapist needs new ideas or directions. She asks a therapist to physically move into another chair and imaginatively take up the position of the person with whom they are working.

The therapist 'introduces' the client to the supervisor, and others if there is a group, imagining that the client is present in the room. This 'helps to avoid theorising or using psychological or detached descriptions of people's experiences' (p. 4). 'I wanted therapists to experience a sense of "extra-vision",' she says, by creating 'a spiral-like discovery process in which we were narrating or story-making in the present moment' (pp. ix–x). This approach, she says, is a development of the Milan group's 'circular' or 'relationship questions' (p. 112), which explore the interactions between therapist, client and the important relationships in the client's life (Cecchin 1987; Hedges 2005; Selvini Palazzoli et al. 1980).

I briefly explained this idea and Tessa readily agreed to try it.

'What if you spoke as if you were Tom and I spoke as if I were you, maybe we could generate some new ideas?'

'So, Tom,' I asked Tessa, 'I'm wondering who in your life is important to you?'

Tessa (as Tom) replied: 'My parents I guess.'

'What ideas do you think your parents have about your life right now?' I asked Tessa (as Tom).

'They always say "whatever makes you happy",' Tessa (as Tom) said. 'But if I got a job and a girlfriend I think they'd be happier. I don't think I've succeeded anywhere.'

'And when your mum sent you that parcel, what do you think was in her mind? What do you think her intentions might have been?'

'Perhaps . . . she wanted to give me something . . . ?'

'What might she have wanted to give you?' I asked.

'Something to help me get the confidence to date girls . . .'

I noticed that Tessa's responses were more thoughtful than they had been.

'OK,' I said. 'Can we switch back now? How do you think this might help in your next conversation with Tom?'

'Well, his mum suggested counselling. I think she found it helpful herself. She wants him to feel better.'

'And he finds it helpful talking to you?'

'Yes.'

'How d'you think you're enabling him to do that?'

'Listening . . . yeah . . .' Tessa said, thoughtfully, 'accepting him . . . and what he says.'

'I'm really interested to hear what it was like for you,' I said, 'when you were answering as if you were Tom.'

'It was really strange,' she said, 'just by being in Tom's shoes and you asking about what his mum might have meant by sending him the parcel and the card helped me understand both of them. Speaking as Tom, it helped me understand him better. And it gave me a different perspective on his mum. I feel better about her.'

'It was fascinating,' I said, 'when you were speaking in Tom's voice you actually came up with that new way of seeing things, how it might be from his mum's point of view.'

Tessa was able to shift from the earlier blaming position towards Tom's mother.

'Now I've had an idea.' Tessa said. 'I don't feel I have to fix things for people. Just by asking these kinds of questions and y'know, being less active, doing less when I'm with the client makes me realise I am actually doing something. I remember you telling me to match my tone and pace with the client's. I feel better now.'

Tessa's style was active; she was 'a do-er'. She wanted practical ways to talk to Tom. Now she had learned how to ask circular/relationship questions that explored clients' relationships with the important people in their lives.

As Tessa and I were co-constructing Tom's identity and his relationships we were also co-constructing our relationship together. 'I've noticed how much more self-reflexive you've become during our conversation,' I said. I wanted to check out whether the supervision was helping. 'Is it going in the way you want?' I asked.

Supervisors can use 'relational reflexivity' (Burnham 1993) to check out how the conversation is going, as we do with clients, asking checking-out questions.

'When you tell me what you're thinking, it helps me to feel safe,' she answered. 'I can tell you things and you let me know what you're thinking . . . I do want to learn, to get better . . . you keep me thinking, reflecting, processing . . . It's not easy . . . you make me work . . . but I always feel energised.'

I felt relieved and pleased, and risked offering a bit more teaching. 'In this way of working we think about the consequences of what we are saying and doing, not just on the client but also on the important people in their life. After all, Tom's relationship with his mum will still continue long after he's stopped seeing you.'

And now she broke in, 'I remember that my mum gave me a book on relationships when I got engaged. I didn't feel humiliated. I thought it was kind of her and it was a useful book.'

At the end of the conversation she said, 'This is a bit like playing chess. It's given me tools. I understand what you were trying to get across about the social, and y'know, how language creates . . . This is a fast way of working.'

Reflexive questions

As a supervisor, notice the contexts and systems to which you are connected:

- Reflect on the 'rules' and language of each system.
- How comfortable are you with taking a 'second order' position as well as a 'first order' position?
- What would encourage you to explore the impact of a therapist's personal or professional stories on the therapy?
- What would encourage you to offer a personal or professional story of your own?
- How do you negotiate offering direct teaching?

BIBLIOGRAPHY

Andersen, T. (1987) 'Reflecting Teams: Dialogue and Meta-dialogue in Clinical Work', *Family Process*, 26(4), 415–28.

Andersen, T. (ed.) (1990) *The Reflecting Team: Dialogues and Dialogues and Dialogues* (Broadstairs: Borgman).

Andersen, T. (1991) 'A Collaboration of Some Called Psychotherapy: Bonds Filled of Expressions, and Expressions Filled of Meaning', draft paper.

Andersen, T. (1992) 'Reflections on Reflecting with Families', in McNamee, S. and Gergen, K. (eds), *Therapy as Social Construction* (London, Newbury Park and New Delhi: Sage), pp. 54–68.

Andersen, T. (1993) 'See, Hear, and be Seen and Heard', in Friedman, S. (ed.), *The New Language of Change: Constructive Collaboration in Psychotherapy* (New York: Guilford Press).

Andersen, T. (1996) 'Researching Client–Therapist Relationships: a Collaborative Study for Informing Therapy', *Journal of Strategic and Systemic Therapies*, 16(2), 125–33.

Andersen, T. (1998) One sentence of five lines about creating meaning, in 'Perspective of Relationship, Prejudice and Bewitchment', *Human Systems: The Journal of Systemic Consultation and Management*, 9(2), 73–80.

Anderson, H. (1997) *Conversation, Language, and Possibilities: A Postmodern Approach to Therapy* (New York: Basic Books).

Asay, T. and Lambert, M. (1999) 'The Empirical Case for the Common Factors in Therapy', in Hubble, M. A., Duncan, B. L. and Miller, S. D., *The Heart and Soul of Change: What Works in Therapy* (Washington: American Psychological Society), pp. 23–55.

Averill, J. (1982) *Anger and Aggression: An Essay on Emotion* (New York: Springer Verlag).

Averill, J. (1992) *Voyages of the Heart: Living an Emotionally Creative Life* (New York: Free Press).

Averill, J. (1996) 'Intellectual Emotions', in Harré, R. and Parrott, W. G., *The Emotions: Social, Cultural, and Biological Dimensions* (London: Sage), pp. 24–38.

Bakhtin, M. (1981) 'Discourse in the Novel', trans. C. Emerson and M. Holquist, in Holquist, M. (ed.), *The Dialogic Imagination: Four Essays by M. M. Bakhtin* (Austin, TX: University of Texas Press).

Bakhtin, M. (1984) *Problems of Dostoevsky's Poetics*, trans. and ed. C. Emerson (Minneapolis and London: University of Minneapolis Press).

Bakhtin, M. (1986) *Speech Genres and Other Late Essays*, trans. Vern W. McGee and ed. C. Emerson and M. Holquist (Austin, TX: University of Texas Press).

Bakhtin, M. (1993) *Towards a Philosophy of the Act*, trans. and notes by V. Lianpov, ed. M. Holquist (Austin, TX: University of Texas Press).

Bateson, G. (1972) *Steps to an Ecology of Mind* (London: Ballantine Books).

Bateson, G. (1979) *Mind and Nature: A Necessary Unity* (Glasgow: Fontana/Collins).

Bateson, G. (1991) *A Sacred Unity – Further Steps to an Ecology of Mind* (New York: HarperCollins).

Becker, H. (1973) *Outsiders: Studies in the Sociology of Deviance* (New York: Free Press).

Bernard, J. and Goodyear, R. (1992) *Fundamentals of Clinical Supervision* (Boston, MA: Allyn & Bacon).

Bird, J. (2006) *Constructing the Narrative in Super-vision* (Auckland, New Zealand: Edge Press).

Boscolo, L. and Bertrando, P. (1996) *Systemic Therapy with Individuals* (London: Karnac Books).

Bowen, M. (1978) *Family Therapy in Clinical Practice* (New York: Jason Aronson).

Boyd-Franklin, N. (1989) *Black Families in Therapy: A Multisystems Approach* (New York and London: Guilford Press).

Brown, L. S. (1994) *Subversive Dialogues: Theory in Feminist Therapy* (New York: Basic Books).

Burnham, J. (1993) 'Systemic Supervision: the Evolution of Reflexivity in the Context of the Supervisory Relationship', *Human Systems*, 4 (Special Issue, 3 & 4), pp. 349–81.

Burnham, J. (2005) 'Relational Reflexivity: a Tool for Socially Constructing Therapeutic Relationships', in Flaskas, C., Mason, B. and Perlesz, A. (eds), *The Space Between: Experience, Context, and Process in the Therapeutic Relationship* (London: Karnac Books).

Burnham, J. and Harris, Q. (2002) 'Cultural Issues in Supervision', in Campbell, D. and Mason, B. (eds), *Perspectives on Supervision* (London and New York: Karnac Books).

Carpenter, H. (2006) 'Reconceptualizing Communication Competence: High Performing Coordinated Communication Competence: a Here-Dimensional View', PhD dissertation, Fielding Graduate University, Santa Barbara, CA.

Carroll, M. (1996) *Counseling Supervision: Theory, Skills and Practice* (London and New York: Cassell).

Casement, P. (1985) *On Learning from the Patient* (London and New York: Tavistock Publications).

Cecchin, G. (1987) 'Hypothesising, Circularity and Neutrality Revisited: an Invitation to Curiosity', *Family Process*, 26(4), 405–13.

Cecchin, G. et al. (1992) *Irreverence: A Strategy for Therapists' Survival* (London: Karnac Books).

Cecchin, G., Lane, G. and Ray, W. A. (1994) *The Cybernetics of Prejudices in the Practice of Psychotherapy* (London: Karnac Books).

Charney, D. S. (2004) 'Psychobiological Mechanisms of Resilience and Vulnerability: Implications for Successful Adaptation to Extreme Stress', *American Journal of Psychiatry*, 161(2), 195–216.

Chidgey, M. 'Exploring Empathy as an Aspect in the Construction of the Therapeutic Relationship', unpublished dissertation, KCC Foundation, London.

Cooperrider, D. L. (1990) 'Positive Image, Positive Action: the Affirmative Basis of Organizing', in Srivastva, S. and Cooperrider, D., *Appreciative Management and Leadership* (San Francisco: Jossey-Bass).

Corrigall, J. and Wilkinson, H. (eds) (2003) *Revolutionary Connections: Psychotherapy and Neuroscience* (London and New York: Karnac Books).

Cronen, V. (1990) 'Co-ordinated Management of Meaning: Practical Theory for the

Complexities and Contradictions of Everyday Life', in Siegfried, J. (ed.), *The Status of Common Sense in Psychology* (Greenwich, CT: Ablex Press).

Cronen, V. (1994) 'Coordinated Management of Meaning: Theory for the Complexities and Contradictions of Everyday Life', in Siegfried, J. (ed.), *The Status of Common Sense in Psychology* (Norwood, NJ: Ablex), 183–207.

Cronen, V. (2000) 'Practical Theory, Practical Art, and the Naturalistic Account of Inquiry', Conference paper for Baylor University.

Cronen, V. (2003) at KCC Workshop 'Coordinated Management of Meaning', London.

Cronen, V. (2004) 'Something Old, Something New: CMM and Mass Communication', *Human Systems*, 15, 167–78.

Cronen, V. (2007) *personal communication* at KCC Workshop, London.

Cronen, V. and Chetro-Szivos, J. (2002) 'Consummatory Moments and Moral Order in Organizational Life', in Meisner, T. (ed.), *A Symphony of Appreciation* (Copenhagen: Danish Psychology Press).

Cronen, V. and Lang, P. (1994) 'Language and Action: Wittgenstein and Dewey in the Practice of Theory and Consultation', *Human Systems*, 5(1–2), 5–45.

Cronen, V., Pearce, W. B. and Xi, C. (1989/90) 'The Meaning of "Meaning" in the CMM Analysis of Communication: a Comparison of Two Traditions', *Research on Language and Social Interaction*, 23, 1–40.

Csordas, T. (2002) *Body/Meaning/Healing* (Basingstoke: Palgrave Macmillan).

Dallos, R. and Draper, R. (2000) *An Introduction to Family Therapy: Systemic Theory and Practice* (Buckingham: Open University Press).

Damascio, A. (2006) *Descartes' Error* (London: Vintage Books).

Darwin, C. (1872) *The Expression of the Emotions in Man and Animals*, reissued (Chicago: University of Chicago Press, 1965).

Davidson, R. J. (2003) 'Affective Neuroscience and Psychophysiology: Towards a Synthesis', *Psychophysiology*, 40(5), 655–65.

Davies, C. A. (1999) *Reflexive Ethnography* (London: Routledge).

Derrida, J. (1998) *Resistances of Psychoanalysis* (Stanford, CA: Stanford University Press).

Dewey, J. (1910) *How we Think* (Boston, New York, Chicago: D. C. Heath).

Dewey, J. (1934) *Art as Experience* (New York: Penguin Group).

Dewey, J. (1958) *Experience and Nature*, 2nd edition (New York: Dover).

Donne, J. (1624) *Meditation, No. 17: Devotions upon Emergent Occasions*.

Duck, S. (1983) *Friends for Life* (Brighton: Harvester).

Einstein, A. (1931) *Cosmic Religion: With Other Opinions and Aphorisms* (New York: Covici-Freide).

Ekman, P. and Friesen, W. V. (1975) *Unmasking the Face: A Guide to Recognizing Emotions from Facial Clues* (Englewood Cliffs, NJ: Prentice Hall).

Elkaim, M. (1990) *If You Love Me, Don't Love Me* (New York: Basic Books).

Fernando, S. (1991) *Mental Health, Race and Culture* (Basingstoke: Macmillan Education; London: Mind Publications).

Festinger, L. et al. (1950) *Social Pressures in Informal Groups: A Study of Human Factors in Housing* (New York: Harper & Row).

Fleuridas, C., Nelson, T. S. and Posenthal, D. M. (1986) 'The Evolution of Circular Questions: Training Family Therapists', *Journal of Marital and Family Therapy*, 12(2), 113–27.

Fliess, W. (1942) 'The Metapsychology of the Analyst', *Psychoanalytic Quarterly*, 11, 211–27.

Foucault, M. (1988) 'Technologies of the Self', in Martin, L., Gutman, L. H. and Hutton, P. (eds), *Technologies of the Self* (Amherst, MA: University of Massachusetts Press).

Frank, J. D. and Frank, J. B. (1991) *Persuasion and Healing*, 3rd edition (Baltimore: Johns

Hopkins University Press).

Fredman, G. (2004) *Transforming Emotion: Conversations in Counselling and Psychotherapy* (London and Philadelphia: Whurr Publishers).

Freire, P. (1992) *Pedagogy of Hope: Reliving Pedagogy of the Oppressed* (New York: Continuum).

Freud, S. (1953–74) *The Complete Psychological Works of Sigmund Freud*, Standard Edition, ed. James Strachey et al. (London: The Hogarth Press and the Institute of Psychoanalysis).

Fruggeri, L. (2002) 'Different Levels of Analysis in the Supervisory Process', in Campbell, D. and Mason, B. (eds), *Perspectives on Supervision* (London and New York: Karnac Books) pp. 3–20.

Gadamer, H-G. (1987) *Philosophical Hermeneutics* (Berkeley, CA: University of California Press).

Garfinkle, H. (1967) *Studies in Ethnomethodology* (Englewood Cliffs, NJ: Prentice Hall).

Geertz, C. (1983) *Local Knowledge: Further Essays in Interpretive Anthropology* (New York: Basic Books).

Geertz, C. (1986) 'On the Nature of Anthropological Understanding', *American Scientist*, 63, 43–57.

Gergen, K. J. (1991) *The Saturated Self* (New York: Basic Books).

Gergen, K. J. (1999) *An Invitation to Social Constructionism* (London: Sage).

Gergen, K. J. (2001) *Social Construction in Context* (London: Sage).

Gibney, P. (1994) 'Time in the Therapeutic Domain', *Australian and New Zealand Journal of Family Therapy*, 15(2), 61–72.

Griffith, J. L., Elliott Griffith, M. and Slovik, L. S. (1990) 'Mind–Body Problems in Family Therapy: Contrasting First- and Second-Order Cybernetics Approaches', *Family Process*, 29 (March), 13–28.

Griffith, J. L. and Griffith, M. E. (1994) *The Body Speaks: Therapeutic Dialogues for Mind–Body Problems* (New York: Basic Books).

Gross, V. (2002) 'Family Therapy Supervision in the Context of an Inpatient Child and Adolescent Eating-disorders Unit', Campbell, D. and Mason, B. (eds), *Perspectives on Supervision* (London and New York: Karnac Books), pp. 117–140.

Guannes, C. and Rasera, E. F. (2006) 'Therapy as Social Construction: an Interview with Sheila McNamee', *Journal of Psychology*, 40(1), 127–36.

Harré, R. (1995) 'Discursive Psychology', in Smith, J. A., Harré, R. and van Langenhove, K. (eds), *Rethinking Psychology* (London: Sage).

Harré, R. (1998) *The Singular Self* (London: Sage).

Harré, R. (2006) *Key Thinkers in Psychology* (London, Thousand Oaks, and New Delhi: Sage Publications).

Harré, R. (2008) *personal communication* at KCC Workshop, London.

Harré, R. and Gillett, G. (1994) *The Discursive Mind* (Thousand Oaks, CA: Sage).

Harré, R. and Parrott, W. G. (1996) *The Emotions: Social, Cultural, and Biological Dimensions* (London: Sage).

Harré, R. and Moghaddam, F. (eds) (2003) *The Self and Others: Positioning Individuals and Groups in Personal, Political, and Cultural Contexts* (Westport, CT and London: Praeger).

Harré, R. and Tissaw, M. (2005) *Wittgenstein and Psychology: A Practical Guide* (Aldershot and Burlington, VT: Ashgate).

Harré, R. and van Langenhove, L. (eds) (1999) *Positioning Theory* (Oxford: Blackwell).

Hayley, J. (1973) *Uncommon Therapy: The Psychiatric Techniques of Milton H. Erikson* (New York and London: W. W. Norton).

Hedges, F. (2000) 'Transforming a University Counselling Service', *Human Systems*, 11, 51–65.

Hedges, F. (2005) *An Introduction to Systemic Therapy with Individuals: A Social Constructionist Approach* (Basingstoke and New York: Palgrave Macmillan).

Hedges, F. and Lang, S. (1993) 'Mapping Personal and Professional Stories', *Human Systems*, 4, 277–98.

Held, B. (1991) 'The Process/Content Distinction Revisited'. *Psychotherapy*, 28, 207–18.

Hoffman, L. (1981) *Foundations of Family Therapy: A Conceptual Framework for Change* (New York: Basic Books).

Hoffman, L. (1985) 'Beyond Power and Control: Towards a "Second-order" Family Systems Therapy', *Family Systems Medicine*, 3(4), 381–96.

Holloway, W. (1984) 'Gender Difference and the Production of Subjectivity', in Henriques, J. et al. (eds), *Changing the Subject* (London: Methuen).

Holt, J. (1989) *Learning All the Time* (New York: Perseus Books).

Hubble, M. A., Duncan, B. L. and Miller, S. D. (1999) *The Heart and Soul of Change: What Works in Therapy* (Washington: American Psychological Society).

Hunt, C. and Sampson, F. (2006) *Writing: Self and Reflexivity* (Basingstoke and New York: Palgrave Macmillan).

James, W. (1884) 'What is an Emotion?' *Mind*, 9, 188–205.

Jones, E. (1993) *Family Systems Therapy* (Chichester, New York, Brisbane and Singapore: John Wiley & Sons).

Jourard, S. M. (1971) *Self-disclosure: An Experimental Analysis of the Transparent Self* (New York: Wiley-Interscience).

Katz, A. and Shotter, J. (1996) 'Articulating a Practice from Within the Practice Itself: Establishing Formative Dialogues by the Use of a "Social Poetics"', *Concepts and Transformation*, 1, 2/3.

Kearney, R. (ed.) (1996) *Paul Ricoeur: The Hermeneutics of Action* (London, Thousand Oaks, New Delhi: Sage Publications).

Keats, J. (1947) *The Letters of John Keats*, Letter 32, ed. M. Forman (London: Oxford University Press), p. 72.

Keedwell, P. (2008) *How Sadness Survived: The Evolutionary Basis of Depression* (Abingdon: Radcliffe Publishing).

Krause, I-B. (1998) *Therapy Across Culture* (London, Thousand Oaks, New Delhi: Sage Publications).

Kristeva, J. (1984) *Revolution in Poetic Language*, trans. L. S. Roudiez (New York: Columbia University Press).

Lakoff, G. and Kovecses, Z. (1983) 'The Cognitive Model of Anger Inherent in American English', *Berkeley Cognitive Science Report*, No. 10 (Berkeley: University of California Press).

Lanamann, J. (1988) 'Social Construction and Materiality: the Limits of Interdeterminacy in Therapeutic Setting', *Family Process*, 37, 392–413.

Lane, C. (2007) *Shyness: How Normal Behaviour Became a Sickness* (New Haven, CT and London: Yale University Press).

Lang, P. (2003) *personal communication.*

Lang, P. (2006) *personal communication.*

Lang, P. (2007) *personal communication.*

Lang, P. (2008) *personal communication.*

Lang, P. (2009) *personal communication.*

Lang, P., Little, M. and Cronen, V. E. (1990) 'The Systemic Professional: Domains of Action and the Question of Neutrality', *Human Systems*, 1, 39–56.

Lang, P. and McAdam, E. (1995) 'Stories, Giving Accounts and Systemic Descriptions', *Human Systems*, 6(2), 1–103.

Lakoff, G. and Johnson, M. (1999) *Philosophy in the Flesh* (New York: Basic Books).

Leppington, R. (1991) 'From Constructivism to Social Constructionism and Doing Critical Therapy', *Human Systems*, 2, 79–103.

Link, B. et al. (1989) 'A Modified Labelling Theory Approach to Mental Disorders: an Empirical Assessment', *American Sociological Review*, 54(3), 400–23.

Lutz, C. A. (1996) 'Engendered Emotion: Gender, Power and the Rhetoric of Emotional Control in American Discourse', in Harré, R. and Parrott, W. G. (eds), *The Emotions: Social, Cultural and Biological Dimensions* (London, Thousand Oaks and Delhi: Sage Publications), pp. 151–70.

Lyotard, J-F. (2001) *The Postmodern Condition*, trans. G. Bennington and B. Masumi (Manchester: Manchester University Press).

Malik, R. and Krause, I-B. (2005) 'Before and Beyond Words: Embodiment and Intercultural Therapeutic Relationships in Family Therapy', in Flaskas, C. et al. (eds), *The Space Between: Experience, Context, and Process in the Therapeutic Relationship* (London: Karnac Books), pp. 95–110.

Mason, B. (2005) 'Relational Risk-taking and the Therapeutic Relationship', in Flaskas, C. et al., *The Space Between: Experience, Context, and Process in the Therapeutic Relationship* (London and New York: Karnac Books).

Maturana, H. (1983) 'What Is It to See?' *Archivos de Biología y Medicina Experimentales*, 16, 135–55.

Maturana, H. and Varela, F. (1987) *The Tree of Knowledge: The Biological Roots of Human Understanding* (Boston: New Science Library/Shambala).

McAdam, E. and Lang, P. (2006) 'Voices of Reconciliation', *Human Systems*, 17, 81–105.

McAdam, E. and Lang, P. (2009) *Appreciative Work in Schools: Generating Future Communities* (Chichester: Kingsham Press).

McCarthy, I. and Byrne, N. (1988) 'Mis-taken Love: Conversations on the Problem of Incest in an Irish Context', *Family Process*, 19, 181–99.

McDaniel, S. et al. (eds) (1997) *The Shared Experience of Illness: Stories of Patients, Families, and Their Therapists* (New York: Basic Books).

McGoldrick, M. (1995) *You Can Go Home Again: Reconnecting with Your Family* (New York and London: W. W. Norton).

McNamee, S. and Gergen, K. J. (eds) (1992) *Therapy as Social Construction* (London: Sage).

McNamee, S. and Gergen, K. J. and associates (1999) *Relational Responsibility* (Thousand Oaks, CA: Sage).

Mead, G. H. (1934) *Mind, Self and Society*, ed. Charles Morris (Chicago: University of Chicago Press).

Merton, R. K. (1948) 'The Self-Fulfilling Prophecy', *Antioch Review* (Summer), 193–210.

Moghaddam, F. (1999) 'Reflexive Positioning: Culture and Private Discourse', in Harré, R. and van Langenhove, L. (eds), *Positioning Theory* (Oxford: Blackwell).

Najavits, l. M. and Strupp, H. H. (1994) 'Differences in the Effectiveness of Psychodynamic Therapists: a Process-outcome Study, *Psychotherapy*, 57, 114–23.

Nightingale, D. and Cromby, J. (eds) (1999) *Social Constructionist Psychology: A Critical Analysis of Theory and Practice* (Buckingham: Open University Press).

Oatley, K. (1996) 'Emotions: Communications to the Self and Others', in Harré, R. and Parrott, W. G. (eds), *The Emotions: Social, Cultural and Biological Dimensions* (London, Thousand Oaks and Delhi: Sage Publications).

Oatley, K. (1996) *Emotions: A Brief History* (Malden: Blackwell).

Ong, W. J. (1982) *Orality and Literacy: The Technologizing of the Word* (London: Routledge).

Oxford English Dictionary (*OED*) (1989) 2nd edition, prepared by J. A. Simpson and E. S. C. Weiner (Oxford: Oxford University Press).

Partridge, K. (2007) 'The Positioning Compass: a Tool to Facilitate Reflexive Positioning', *Human Systems*, 18, 96–111.

Pearce, W. B. (1989) *Communication and the Human Condition* (Carbondale, IL: University of Southern Illinois Press).

Pearce, W. B. (1994) *Interpersonal Communication: Making Social Worlds* (London: HarperCollins).

Pearce, W. B. (1999) 'Using CMM: The Coordinated Management of Meaning', Pearce Associates Seminar: San Mateo, California.

Pearce, W. B. (2007) *Making Social Worlds: A Communication Perspective* (Oxford and Victoria, Australia: Blackwell).

Pearce, W. B. and Cronen, V. (1980) *Communication, Action, and Meaning: The Creation of Social Realities* (New York: Praeger).

Perry, R. (1993) 'Empathy – Still at the Heart of Therapy: the Interplay of Context and Empathy', *Australian and New Zealand Journal of Family Therapy*, 14(2), 63–74.

Qualley, D. (1997) *Turns of Thought: Teaching Composition as Reflexive Inquiry* (London: Heinemann).

Ricoeur, P. (1972) 'Metaphor and the Central Problem of Hermeneutics', *Revue philosophique de Louvain*, 70, 93–112, trans. and ed. J. B. Thompson, in *Hermeneutics and the Human Sciences* (Cambridge: Cambridge University Press).

Rober, P. (1999) 'The Therapist's Inner Conversation in Family Therapy Practice: Some Ideas about the Self of the Therapist, Therapeutic Impasse, and the Process of Reflection', *Family Process*, 38(2), 209–28.

Roberts, J. (2005) 'Transparency and Self-Disclosure in Family Therapy: Dangers and Possibilities', *Family Process*, 44(1), 45–63.

Rogers, C. (1957) 'The Necessary and Sufficient Conditions of Therapeutic Personality Change', in Kirschenbaum, H. and Henderson, V. L. (eds), *The Carl Rogers Reader* (1990) (London: Constable).

Rogers, C. (1986) 'A Client-centred/Person-centred Approach to Therapy', in Kirschenbaum, H. and Henderson, V. L. (eds), *The Carl Rogers Reader* (1990) (London: Constable).

Roper-Hall, A. (1997) 'Working Systemically with Older People and their Families who have "Come to Grief"', in Sutcliffe, P. et al (eds), *Working with the Dying and Bereaved* (London: Macmillan).

Rosaldo, M. (1977) 'The Rhetoric of Control: Ilongots viewed as Natural Bandits and Wild Indians', in Babcock, B. (ed.), *The Reversible World: Symbolic Inversion in Art and Society* (Ithaca, NY: Cornell University Press), pp. 240–57.

Rosen, S. (ed.) (1982) *My Voice Will Go With You: The Teaching Tales of Milton H. Erikson* (New York and London: W. W. Norton).

Sapolsky, R. M. (1988) *Why Zebras Don't Get Ulcers: An Updated Guide to Stress, Stress-related Diseases and Coping* (New York: W. H. Freeman).

Scheff, T. (1966) *Being Mentally Ill* (Chicago: Aldine).

Schon, D. A. (1987) *Educating the Reflective Practitioner* (San Francisco, CA: Jossey-Bass).

Selvini Palazzoli, M., Boscolo, L., Cecchin, G. and Prata, G. (1978) *Paradox and Counter-paradox: A New Model in the Therapy of the Family in Schizophrenic Transaction*, trans. E. V. Burt (New York: Jason Aronson).

Selvini Palazzoli, M., Boscolo, L., Cecchin, G. and Prata, G. (1980) 'Hypothesising, Circularity and Neutrality: Three Guidelines for the Conductor of the Session', *Family Process*, 19(1), 3–12.

Shilling, C. (2003) *The Body and Social Theory* (London: Sage).

Shotter, J. (1993) *Conversational Realities: Constructing Life through Language* (London: Sage).

Shotter, J. (2004) *On the Edge of Constructionism: 'Withness'-Thinking Versus 'Aboutness'-Thinking* (London: KCC Foundation).

Shotter, J. (2005) *Wittgenstein in Practice: His Philosophy of Beginnings, and Beginnings and Beginnings* (London: KCC Foundation).

Shotter, J. (2007) 'Not to Forget Tom Andersen's *Way* of being Tom Andersen: the Importance of what "Just Happens" to Us', paper delivered at the 12th International Meeting on the Treatment of Psychosis, in Palanga, Lithuania, 29 August–2 September.

Smale, G. G. (1977) *Prophecy, Behaviour and Change: An Examination of Self-fulfilling Prophecies in Helping Relationships* (London, Henley and Boston: Routledge & Kegan Paul).

Snyder, C. R., Michael, S. and Cheavens, J. (1999) 'Hope as a Psychotherapeutic Foundation of Common Factors, Placebos and Expectations', in Hubble, M. A. et al., *The Heart and Soul of Change: What Works in Therapy* (Washington: American Psychological Society).

Solms, M. and Turnbull, O. (2002) *The Brain and the Inner World: An Introduction to the Neuroscience of Subjective Experience* (New York: Other Press).

Srivastva, S. and Cooperrider, D. L. (1999) *Appreciative Management and Leadership: The Power of Positive Thought and Action in Organizations* (Euclid, OH: Williams Custom Publishing).

Stearns, P. N. and Knapp, M. (1996) 'Historical Perspectives on Grief', in Harré, R. and Parrott, W. G., *The Emotions: Social, Cultural, and Biological Dimensions* (London: Sage), pp. 132–50.

Stout, J. (1988) *Ethics After Babel: The Languages of Morals and their Discontents* (Boston, MA: Beacon Press).

Tallman, K. and Bohart, A. (1999) 'The Client as the Common Factor: Clients as Self-Healers', in Hubble, M. A. et al., *The Heart and Soul of Change: What Works in Therapy* (Washington: American Psychological Society).

Thomas, W. and Swaine Thomas, D. (1928) *The Child in America: Behavior Problems and Programs* (New York: Knopf).

Varela, F. (1975) 'A Calculus for Self-reference', *International Journal of General Systems*, 2, 5–24.

Varela, F. (1988) 'Les multiples figures de la circularité', *Cahiers critiques de thérapie familial et de practiques de réseaux*, 9, 45–8.

von Foerster, H. (1984) 'On Constructing a Reality', in Prieser, W. W. (ed.), *Environmental Design Research*, 2 (Stroudsburg, PA: Dowden, Hutchinson & Ross).

von Glaserfeld, E. (1984) 'An Introduction to Radical Constructivism', in Watzlawick, P. (ed.), *The Invented Reality* (New York: W. W. Norton).

Vygotsky, L. S. (1962) *Thought and Language* (Cambridge, MA: MIT Press; originally published in Russian in 1934).

Vygotsky, L. S. (1966) 'Development of Higher Mental Functions', in Leontyev, A. N., Luria, A. R. and Smirnov, A. (eds), *Psychological Research in the USSR* (Moscow: Progress Publishers).

Vygotsky, L. S. (1978) *Mind in Society: The Development of Higher Psychological Processes*, ed. M. Cole et al. (Cambridge, MA: Harvard University Press).

Vygotsky, L. S. (1986) *Thought and Language*, trans. and newly revised by Alex Kozulin (Cambridge, MA: MIT Press; originally published in Russian in 1934).

Wade, A. (1997) 'Small Acts of Living: Everyday Resistance to Violence and Other Forms of Oppression', *Contemporary Family Therapy*, 19(1), 23–39.

Watzlawick, P. (1984) *The Invented Reality* (New York: W. W. Norton).

Weingarten, K. (2007) 'Hope in a Time of Global Despair', in Flaskas, C. et al. (eds), *Hope and Despair in Narrative and Family Therapy: Adversity, Forgiveness and Reconciliation* (Hove and New York: Routledge).

White, M. (1995) 'Reflecting Teamwork as Definitional Ceremony', in White, M. (ed.), *Re-Authoring Lives: Interviews and Essays* (Adelaide, Australia: Dulwich Centre Publications).

White, M. (1997) *Narratives of Therapists' Lives* (Adelaide: Dulwich Centre Publications).

White, M. (2007) *Maps of Narrative Practice* (New York: W. W. Norton).

Wilkinson, M. (1992) 'How do we Understand Empathy Systemically?' *Journal of Family Therapy*, 14, 193–205.

Wilson, J. (2007) *The Performance of Practice* (London: Karnac Books).

Wittgenstein, L. (1953) *Philosophical Investigations* (Oxford: Blackwell).

Wittgenstein, L. (1981) *Zettel*, 2nd edition, ed. G. E. N. Anscombe and G. H. V. Wright (Oxford: Blackwell).

Wright, E. R. et al. (2000) 'Deinstitutionalization, Social Rejection and the Self-esteem of Former Mental Patients', *Journal of Health and Social Behavior*, 41(1), 68–90.

INDEX

10010756R00102

Printed in Great Britain
by Amazon